Wednesday Wonderings

Wednesday Wonderings

Spiritual Journaling Through a Lens

GARY E. NELSON

RESOURCE *Publications* • Eugene, Oregon

WEDNESDAY WONDERINGS
Spiritual Journaling Through a Lens

Copyright © 2012 Gary E. Nelson. All rights reserved. Except for brief quotations in critical publications or reviews, no part of this book may be reproduced in any manner without prior written permission from the publisher. Write: Permissions. Wipf and Stock Publishers, 199 W. 8th Ave., Suite 3, Eugene, OR 97401.

All scripture quotations in this publication are from the Good News Translation in Today's English Version—Second Edition Copyright © 1992 by American Bible Society. Used by Permission.

Resource Publications
An Imprint of Wipf and Stock Publishers
199 W. 8th Ave., Suite 3
Eugene, OR 97401

www.wipfandstock.com

ISBN 13: 978-1-62032-529-2

Manufactured in the U.S.A.

For all who taught me to wonder, and all who wonder with me.

Contents

Foreword by William Boyd Grove / ix
Acknowledgments / xi
Introduction / xiii

Wednesday Wonderings / 1

Foreword

THE SABBATH IS THE seventh day. However, I have a brief Sabbath In the middle of the week. When my Wednesday morning email arrives, bringing with it Gary Nelson's Wednesday Wonderings for that week, I turn aside from work, as God commanded us to do on the seventh day, and experience rest, renewal and holiness.

The Benedictines gave to us the spiritual practice of Lectio Divina, the praying of the scriptures. Gary Nelson's camera lens leads us to pray the scripture text, which he is illuminating with his camera. Like the parables of Jesus, his artistry with the lens, "opens the scriptures" so that they are not to us words external to us, but words that invade our lives with truth and meaning which become part of us in the deepest places in our hearts.

So, dear friends, I invite you to experience the Sabbath in the middle of the week as you pray the scriptures and invite the holy to move into your souls.

—William Boyd Grove
Bishop, United Methodist Church

Acknowledgments

NOT LONG AFTER I started circulating Wednesday Wonderings some folks began asking, "You are going to publish these as a book, aren't you?" I am grateful for their prodding because without it I probably would not have taken the step to offer this collection as a book. Many have expressed their appreciation for some of the photos and writings that are included in this book. I have been blessed by their affirmations and am grateful.

I want to thank Megan Ann Richardson for her work in converting all my photos from color to black-and-white images. When the publisher told me all my images had to be in black-and-white and prepared a special way for publishing I felt pretty overwhelmed. Megan graciously helped me over that mountain by doing all the conversions for me. I am also grateful to Bishop William Boyd Grove for writing the Forward for the book. I am honored by his words and participation.

Finally, I must thank Patti, my wife, soul-mate, and companion in wandering—and the one who always graciously answers, "Yes, it's okay. Go ahead," when I ask, "Do you mind if I stop and take a picture?" Even after one picture turns into several, she still patiently waits and says, "Yes." No wonder we've wandered and wondered together these past forty years!

Introduction

IF THE "EYES ARE the window for the soul," then I am convinced that the camera lens is the telescope and microscope for the soul. The lens sharpens focus while offering perspective and insight that the eyes alone find more difficult to achieve. Wednesday Wonderings was born when the spiritual hunger of my own soul converged with other needs around the same time.

My journey as a pastor has taken several unexpected twists and turns. I felt affirmed as a parish pastor when I first began a life in ministry after graduating from seminary. I thought the parish was definitely where God was calling me and where I belonged. Four years later I was very surprised when God called me to specialize as a pastoral counselor, taking me away from my home state of West Virginia for many years. More recently, I was just as surprised when God decided it was time for me to return to West Virginia and re-enter parish ministry as the pastor of a church.

As we were preparing to transition back to parish ministry my wife (a hospital nurse for over thirty years) proposed that she work as a traveling nurse for the nine months remaining before I took my next assignment. For the next several months she took a couple of hospital nursing assignments, I took a sabbatical to write a book on teen depression, and together we traveled around much of the United States, having a wonderful time playing and taking hundreds of photos of God's majestic creations.

When we arrived at our new church assignment I framed several of my nature photos and hung them on the wall of my office, telling folks that it was my Spirit Wall. It was not a wall of pretty pictures. Rather, it was a wall of moments, moments when I had stood in wonder and amazement as I gazed upon the majesty of God's creation and experienced a communion of my spirit and the Holy Spirit. Soon I realized I needed more of that sort of spiritual journaling with my camera, so I began to carry my camera with

Wednesday Wonderings

me, just as I had done during our nine months of wandering around the country. Our wandering started my wondering.

Practicing spiritual disciplines is not easy. I've tried several variations over the years, some more successfully than others. Spiritual recipes have never worked for me. Doing something just because it worked for others hasn't proved successful for me. I've always heeded the call of the hymn to, "Take Time to be Holy," but in less traditional ways. I've had to find my own way to have holy time. As I began to wander with my camera and wonder through its lens, I realized a new spiritual discipline had emerged for me.

When we arrived at our new church assignment and I once more began serving as a parish pastor, I felt like I needed some form of communication with my parishioners during the week. Sunday–to–Sunday seemed like too long a time without contact with many of my parishioners. A midweek outreach of some sort seemed like a good idea, and Wednesday was the natural choice. The internet also posed such great outreach potential that I decided to send a weekly email to my parishioners. "What to send?" I thought as I sat at my desk in my office. Then I glanced at my Spirit Wall, and yes, you guessed it, Wednesday Wonderings was born. The email began as an outreach to my parishioners who in turn, sent it on to others as their own form of outreach.

Basically, what you are reading in this book is a collection from the first three years of Wednesday Wonderings. There are enough to last you two years if you read one a week. All of the photos are mine. I try to keep a camera with me so I can take photos during my week. At some point early in each week a photo and a message find their way together. The series still continues each week as an email to my parishioners and as postings on a few blogs and Facebook. If you read this book and would like to continue to receive the series email me at revgenelson@yahoo.com and I will add you to the list of recipients.

This process has already managed to get others watching and wondering. Every now and then someone will say to me, "You know, I saw something the other day that would make a great Wednesday Wonderings," or, "You've got to stop and take a picture of this. It would make a great Wednesday Wonderings." I am deeply thankful to know that my witness has encouraged others to delve into closer relationship with God. I hope this collection of my Wednesday Wonderings will invite you to do some of your own wondering with God.

1

"From the east to the west . . ."

"From the east to the west praise the name of the Lord." (Psalm 113:3)

FROM THE RISING OF the sun in the east to its setting in the west we are to be in praise of the Lord. Praising means focused practiced attention to our relationship with the Lord. Praising means more than just saying, "thank you" (although that's part of it). Praising means living in the awareness that we draw our moment-to-moment essence of life from the one who causes the sun to rise and set. We draw our energy, our hope, our very reason for being from the one who brings light to darkness, order from chaos. If we live in praise of the Lord, we will live in the hope and peace of the Lord. "From the east to the west praise the name of the Lord."

I pray that God will help me lead a life of praise! How about you?

2

"Be tolerant with one another . . ."

". . . there is no longer any distinction between Gentiles and Jews, circumcised and uncircumcised, barbarians, savages, slaves, and free, but Christ is all, Christ is in all. You are the people of God; he loved you and chose you for his own. So then, you must clothe yourselves with compassion, kindness, humility, gentleness, and patience. Be tolerant with one another . . ." (Colossians 3:11–13)

Wednesday Wonderings

Okay, so it's easy to notice our differences, but then what do we do with them? Paul made that pretty clear in his letter to early Christians in Colossae. We are to treat each other with compassion, kindness, humility, gentleness, and patience in an effort to be truly tolerant with one another. As I've been saying recently, it's not so much which side of the issue you're on, but how you treat each other in the debate that will make the difference between community building and community destruction.

There are many critical issues facing our country and world today. Too often I hear us deadlocked not just because of differences of opinion, but rather, because of total intolerance of the other and their opinions. If we are to make progress at solving the myriad of difficulties facing us we must first learn to tolerate one another in the spirit of St. Paul. Then and only then will we build instead of destroy community.

I pray that God will give me the gift to tolerate and cherish others. How about you?

3

"... scolded the people..."

"Some people brought children to Jesus for him to place his hands on them, but the disciples scolded the people. When Jesus noticed this, he was angry and said to his disciples, 'Let the children come to me, and do not stop them, because the Kingdom of God belongs to such as these.'" (Mark 10:13–14)

Wednesday Wonderings

THE DISCIPLES FREQUENTLY MISUNDERSTOOD Jesus and had to be lovingly corrected by their master. In this case, they were about to hurt children by keeping them away from Jesus. The truth of the matter is that it's easy to misunderstand and hurt each other as we act out of our misunderstanding.

As I stood at the counter to purchase our tickets for the tour that would take us to the summit of Mt. Washington in New Hampshire, the lady helping me said, "Oh you're going to love it up there. The view is breathtaking and the *rye mice* are everywhere! There are some that are this big!" She held up her hands to illustrate the eight to ten inch–length of the little creatures. Having traveled to the top of Pike's Peak a few years ago and seen the small mammals that scampered around the rocks at the top of its summit, I made a mental note to myself to be sure and get some pictures of the hardy little creatures that inhabit the barren wilderness of Mt. Washington's summit where winds have been clocked at over 200 miles an hour.

As we neared the summit I began my search for the *rye mice*. When we reached the summit I still had found no *rye mice* so I spent several minutes photographing the beautiful structures in the picture above. The temperature was only eight degrees at the summit. The tour guide told us that these structures are frozen clouds formed when the moisture of the clouds hanging over the summit condenses and freezes under the direction of the harsh winds.

Having failed in my efforts to photograph the illusive small mammals high atop Mt. Washington, my curiosity was aroused, so when I returned to my laptop I began to search for more information about these *rye mice*. I was frustrated in my search until I caught a glimpse of a phrase in an article describing the sights at the top of Mt. Washington. It seems that Mt. Washington is known for its spectacular *rime ice* formations. I misunderstood the ticket agent. I had spent my time disappointingly looking for the illusive *rye mice* while all along I was taking pictures of the beautiful frozen clouds—the *rime ice*.

It's easy to misunderstand, and if we're not careful, to hurt each other in our misunderstanding. I pray for understanding as well as the patience and care not to hurt others in my misunderstanding. How about you?

4

"... I will fear no evil ..."

"Even though I go through the deepest darkness, I will not be afraid, Lord, for you are with me." (Psalm 23:4)

Wednesday Wonderings

Boo! As soon as I snapped this photo and put in on the computer screen I realized where science fiction writers and Hollywood movie makers get a lot of inspiration—from life right around us. If I blew this wasp out of proportion to one hundred times its normal size it could easily pass as the leading character in a science fiction flick entitled, *The Alien Who Ate the Church*.

Painful, tragic things happen not just in the movies but also in real life. We struggle, we survive, and we get through. Yet often times it is fear accompanying our difficulties that can hinder or block our efforts to get through by blowing everything out of proportion. Fear can become almost like a secondary infection that accompanies an accidental wound. The initial wound might not be life-threatening but the accompanying infection might take us to an early grave.

I was living with my family and working as a pastoral counselor in the Washington, D.C metro area during the time when the sniper attacks took place. For several weeks the sniper shot and killed several people at various locations including stores, gas stations, schools, and restaurants. It was a terrible situation. A story relating to the shooting was on the TV or in the newspapers almost every day. It finally reached the point where people were beginning to tell me that they were afraid to go out, or afraid to get out of their cars to pump gas. For some the fear of the sniper was driving them into seclusion or stressing them out. Their fear was blowing everything out of proportion.

I began to remind folks that it was their fear of the sniper that was destroying their lives. I told them that statistically their chances of being killed in a car crash were still higher than being killed by the sniper. I also told them that if every time they turned on their TV there was a little box in the corner of the screen that told them how many folks had died in car crashes that day, some of them would probably let the fear of car crashes keep them from riding in autos ever again.

The stories of the sniper were so present with them in the daily news that they were allowing their fear of the sniper to choke life from them. The good news of the Psalmist is that God is with us, so fear has no power. Bad things happen, but if we allow fear to have a presence, it can become the *evil alien* that threatens to suck the very life from us. Ask God to be present. Practice spending time in the presence of God and fear will be foiled. Where God is present, fear cannot reside.

". . . I will fear no evil . . ."

"Even if I go through the deepest darkness, I will not be afraid, Lord, for you are with me." I do not want fear to rule my life, nor do I want to allow others to use fear to manipulate me. I pray for God's presence with me in the good and not so good so that I will fear no evil. How about you?

5

"We urge you, our friends, to warn . . ."

"We urge you, our friends, to warn the idle, encourage the timid, help the weak, be patient with everyone. See that no one pays back wrong for wrong, but at all times make it your aim to do good to one another and to all people." (I Thessalonians 5:14-15)

"We urge you, our friends, to warn..."

A COUPLE OF YEARS ago Patti and I were driving through one of the western states with our two Boston terriers. It was time for all of us to take a break and stretch our legs, so we pulled into a rest area where it looked as though we could walk our dogs. As we drove into the parking lot we saw the sign in the picture above. We not only heeded the sign's warning by not leaving the sidewalks, we didn't even get out the car and use the sidewalks. Off we went for the next rest stop we could find without such an ominous warning. The truth is that many times we heed warnings, but many times we disregard them. I wonder why we dismiss the well-intentioned warnings of others and then find ourselves falling into the *holes* they warned us to avoid . . .

A couple of days ago Patti and I were driving through a town in Pennsylvania when we both were startled to see a sign by the road that read: *Speed Trap Ahead*. Now stop and think about that for a moment. The same folks who set a trap for us are warning us about the trap? Did the town find that so many folks disregarded the more typical sort of sign that usually reads something like, *Speed Checked by Radar*, that they decided to take pity on the would-be speeders and ticket-receivers by posting a more blatant sign like, *Speed Trap Ahead*? What does it take to get us to pay attention and trust the warnings?

We've almost conditioned our selves to disregard warnings, resulting in our experiencing more hurt and hardship for our selves and others. God sends us many warnings through folks like the Apostle Paul who wrote the message in the letter to the Thessalonians I quoted above. The warnings are intended to build us up and to help us avoid tearing down our selves and others. I pray that God will give me the awareness, good sense, and fortitude to heed the warnings. How about you?

6

"... rejected as worthless..."

"The stone which the builders rejected as worthless turned out to be the most important of all." (Psalm 118:22 and quoted again in Acts 4:11)

"... rejected as worthless..."

Okay, admit it, you've spent untold hours in your yard during the spring and summer trying to rid it of the *dreaded* dandelions! Then, if your neighbor didn't do the same, you probably cast a few dirty looks toward his yard and muttered a few less-than-kind words as his *disgusting yellow weeds* turned to feathery white and proceeded to repopulate your yard with the *awful aliens*. Many a dandelion has known the wrath of the green lawn fancier.

But wait—just this week I read that scientists have discovered a new procedure that will allow them to commercially produce natural latex from dandelions! Apparently this comes just in the nick of time because the rubber tree plantations are being attacked by a new species of fungus threatening to wipe out that source of natural latex. The tiny plant that has spawned a multimillion-dollar lawn pesticide industry aimed at its destruction may turn out to provide the latex necessary for doctor's gloves when they perform surgery in hospitals. Imagine that . . .

There are many persons in our world today that we tend to reject as *worthless* for a variety of reasons, too many for me to go into in this brief offering. Maybe we should learn our lesson from Jesus, the one the Apostle Paul says that was the "rejected stone" which "turned out to be the most important of all." I pray that God will confront, convict, and heal me if ever I look upon another and have any thought of their somehow being *worthless*. How about you?

7

"... but if ..."

"I may be able to speak the languages of human beings and even of angels, but if I have no love, my speech is no more than a noisy gong or a clanging bell. I may have the gift of inspired preaching; I may have all knowledge and understand all secrets; I may have all the faith needed to move mountains—but if I have no love, I am nothing. I may give away everything I have, and even give up my body to be burned—but if I have no love, this does me no good." (I Corinthians 13:1-3)

"... but if..."

ON SEVERAL OCCASIONS I have found myself driving in the predawn hours of the morning, keenly intent on arriving at my destination by the scheduled time. (Why else would I be driving in the predawn hours of the morning?) Then, to my joy and frustration God has decided to throw a *but* into my morning drive. "I really need to get to my destination *but* I can't pass up the opportunity to stop and take a picture of this beautiful sunrise," I say to myself. I get out of the car, and as I'm taking the picture, the picture and the day come into focus. Once again I'm reminded by the sunrise that whatever I do that day everything I do will be influenced by the awareness gained from the sunrise moment—that this day is another gift from God. "Thanks be to God!"

But's are important in our lives. They can function as the interruption we need to help us regain and retain our true focus. I have a piece of paper that simply says, "... *but if*... " framed and sitting in my office as a reminder of what the Apostle Paul meant when he said, "... *but if* I have no love ... " I pray that whenever I find myself focused on any conversation, interaction, agenda, or project I will be interrupted by God whispering Paul's words in my ear, "... *but if* I have no love ..." How about you?

8

"... pruning ..."

"... They will hammer their swords into plows and their spears into pruning knives. Nations will never again go to war, never prepare for battle again." (Isaiah 2:4 and Micah 4:3)

"... pruning..."

A COUPLE OF WEEKS ago I found the large blue Advent candles in one of the church closets and realized that they would need some *pruning* if folks were to be able to see the flickering of the flame over the sides of the candles. The wicks had burned down inside the candles about an inch during the previous Advent season. So, I stood outside the back door of the church and commenced with the *pruning*, leaving a pile of blue wax scattered among the fallen leaves.

Okay, so *pruning* candles may seem like a stretch but you catch my drift. Pruning is essential for some things to work to their fullest capacity. Take grape vines, for example. Pruning is necessary for them to produce abundantly. In an agrarian society like ancient Israel, there were limited resources, especially the precious metals necessary to form pruning hooks. If too much fighting required too much metal to be beaten into swords and spears, then not enough metal was available for plowshares and pruning hooks. Eventually the community's food supply was endangered by the lack of plowshares and pruning hooks, thus threatening the future existence of the community. Resources are precious to the life of any community.

Emotional resources are precious to the life of relationships and the community. It troubles me today to see our willingness to devote so much time, energy, and emotional resources to fighting each other. We seem so intent on tearing each other down, proving the other wrong, or simply despising the other. We have much of our emotional investments in swords and spears, and very little in plowshares and pruning hooks. We seem convinced that we can just keep going at this pace of fighting and hating with no consequences. We cannot survive in healthy relationships and communities with such a distribution of resources. Our fighting and hate will consume the resources we need to build and maintain loving relationships. Eventually our swords and spears won't save us. Instead, they will be the means to our emotional and relational destruction.

In Advent we are called to wait and prepare for the coming Christ child who will lead us in the path of peace. He is the one who calls us to redistribute our resources, to beat our swords into plowshares and our spears into pruning hooks. I pray that God will keep me busy at the anvil beating swords into plowshares and spears into pruning hooks. How about you?

9

"... the spiritual gift that is in you..."

"Do not neglect the spiritual gift that is in you . . ." (I Timothy 4:14)

MUDSICLES—THAT'S WHAT I CALL them. Minerals and mud are gathered as the water trickles down the rocky face, only to be trapped in mid air by the sudden drop of temperature. The minerals trapped inside the ice turn the whole sculpture into a dangling mass of frozen orange water. Minerals, mud, and water are dangling from the edge, waiting to be released with the next thaw.

I spotted these *mudsicles* on the way home from the funeral of a gentleman who briefly had been my pastor while I was in college. He arrived at our church while I was away at college so I barely knew him. One Sunday when I was home from school I attended church with my family. I was majoring in biology in my junior year of school, with a plan to finish and head to medical school. When I shook hands with the pastor at the back of the church I told him that his sermon about *gifts* struck a chord with me because I felt that I had gifts God was calling me to use as a physician. The pastor looked straight at me and said, "God is telling me that you are being called into ministry." Shocked, and somewhat taken aback, I replied, "Gee, I'm sorry, but I'm afraid that you and God have a wrong number." I left and put the whole incident out of my mind. It was only a few months later that God made a direct call to me, summoning me to ordained ministry, and sending me to seminary instead of medical school.

That pastor saw gifts locked inside of me that God was waiting to release before I ever saw them for myself. The Apostle Paul reminds us of spiritual gifts we are given that are waiting to be released and used for the service of Christ. As we anticipate the celebration of the birth of the Christ Child and the gift of God's never-failing love released through him, I pray that God will continue to remind me not to neglect the spiritual gifts God has placed in me for the work of God's Kingdom. How about you?

10

"The light shines in the darkness..."

"The light shines in the darkness, and the darkness has never put it out." (John 1:5)

I THINK FOR ME no greater words of hope have ever been spoken. I have known and suspect that I will yet know times of darkness in my life. I can

"The light shines in the darkness . . ."

no more escape the darkness than the day can escape the night. Yet this is my testimony, "The light shines in the darkness, and the darkness has never put it out." From that experience I draw faith and hope that the darkness will never overcome the light. This Christmas I celebrate once more the coming of God's Light of hope and peace in the presence of God's Christ child. This Light has a lot of work to do in our world. O how we need the Light to cast out the darkness of judgment, hate, and violence. I pray that God will keep me focused on the hope, peace, and work of this Light. How about you?

11

"... completely amazed..."

"They were all completely amazed and praised God, saying, 'We have never seen anything like this!'" (Mark 2:12)

I WAS IN A cemetery early this morning taking a photo of a statue. I was struck by the lonely figure's beauty in the swirling snow. Then, just as I started to open my car door and escape the cold, I noticed one snowflake that had stuck to the housing of my side view mirror. The beauty of the statue paled in the grandeur of God's tiny, amazing creation! It was almost as if God was playing with me a little and saying, "You want to see beauty and wonder? I'll show you beauty and wonder! Here, check out this itsy-bitsy precisely perfect snowflake."

Sometimes I think the world is divided into two kinds of people—those who can be amazed and those who cannot. I'm definitely one of the former. I see and experience so many amazing things that God has prepared for me. These gifts from God send me into a state of awe and wonder—amazement. Sometimes it's the glory of something as simple as a snowflake. Sometimes it's the awareness of once fractured relationships that are now healed. It's an interesting experience, one that reminds me that at heart I am a child, a child of God, enjoying each amazing experience and eagerly anticipating the next one. To be amazed is to be invited momentarily into the majesty of God's love. I forget about the *how*—and simply let go to bask in the *wow*!

How sad it must be to live without amazement. I can't even imagine, but I can invite. I can invite those I meet in that awful state of mind to open their lives to experience God's amazing love. I pray that God will help me always to be open in child-like amazement to the workings of divine love. How about you?

12

"... may your will be done..."

"... may your will be done on earth as it is in heaven." (Matthew 6:10)

By now there are many folks in our part of the east coast who are already tired of the last several days and weeks of biting cold, blowing snow, and frozen roads. When I spoke on *teen depression* at a local high school

"*. . . may your will be done . . .*"

earlier this week some of the students actually admitted they were glad to be back in school after too many boring snow days at home. Had we been in charge, we would not have ordered this kind of weather.

The experts tell us that were it not for the snow packs that melt gradually and allow the water to percolate down into the water tables below, we'd soon find ourselves in a heap of trouble. Apparently for many parts of the country it's these snowfalls we often consider *inconveniences* that can make a difference between food on the table and parched crops dying in the fields. Thank God we're not in charge! We'd order balmy winter temperatures and blue skies until we had starved ourselves to death. With a lack of information and an abundance of personal opinions we would drive ourselves into starvation and extinction.

Maybe it's no different from times past, but today I find that we are often too quick to offer an opinion or judgment as though it's *gospel* even though we lack the data to make a truly informed decision. I watch, as this process seems to lead to more fighting and division instead of dialogue and unity. Why is it so important that we're seen as always being right? It's really okay not to know everything. It's okay to trust that God knows, and that means we don't have to fight about it.

I pray that in the future I will be reminded by God that I don't know, nor do I need to know, everything— and that God will call me instead, to love and trust. How about you?

13

"... shelter and strength..."

"God is our shelter and strength, always ready to help in times of trouble." (Psalm 46:1)

TROUBLE HAPPENS, WHETHER IT comes in the form of a freezing frost-covered morning, a devastating earthquake, or the crushing proclamation

"... *shelter and strength* ..."

in a relationship, "I don't love you anymore." When trouble happens we often find ourselves looking for the *why*. The questions are one way that we express the hurt, fear, and confusion that accompany trouble. Usually, what we need more than *answers* is *shelter*.

Sometimes we need physical shelter like my feathered-friend in the photo, but more often we need spiritual shelter. We need some *place* where we know we can find comfort and a sense that the trouble encompassing us is not the final word for life. In the midst of the trouble we need assurance that life will go on, even if at the present moment we cannot glimpse a picture of life on the far end of the trouble. We need to know there will be an *after*.

Shelter is the place where we can find rest from the turmoil long enough so we can continue to do what is necessary as we work our way through troubled times. The psalmist proclaims how God's daily gift of life is shelter, a promise of the *after*. God has seen him through—the good, the bad, and the ugly. In God's loving embrace the Psalmist finds *shelter*—rest from the confusion and hope for an *after*. From this same experience of God's love we gain the awareness and strength to proclaim, "God is *my* shelter and strength . . ." Then we can offer our warm embrace to others who need *shelter*. I pray that God will give me the sensitivity and courage to be a shelter for others. How about you?

14

"... regard for the law..."

"If you have no regard for the law, you are on the side of the wicked ..." (Proverbs 28:4)

CAN'T YOU JUST HEAR that lead goose honking, "Put the pedal to the metal"? Yeah, and trying to keep them off the grass—good luck! As much as

". . . regard for the law . . ."

we sometimes hate to admit it, rules are important if we're to live in healthy, fulfilling relationships. When couples and families come for counseling, I often hear complaints like, "We're just not compatible," or "We just can't communicate," or, We're just not in love anymore." What I most often find is that they've gotten sloppy with the *rules*.

At some point in their relationship they began to fudge on the *rules*. Instead of taking the time, energy, patience, and discipline to follow some fairly simple rules, they became more impulsive. Throwing caution to the wind they mistook comfort and familiarity for a license to say and do whatever they felt like letting out. The result was the hurt, confusion, and despair that brought them to my office for counseling or *couple's rehab*.

God's *rules* for healthy, fulfilling life and relationships are laid out in different forms in both the Old and New Testaments of the Bible. John Wesley, the founder of Methodism, actually summarized them into 3 simple rules that I'll paraphrase here: 1) Do no harm. 2) Do all the good you can. 3) Stay in love with the Lord. All three rules are critical and interconnected. However, if we focus on the first for just a moment, you can see what I mean by the *fudging* I've seen in so many relationships. If couples use their comfort and familiarity with one another as a license to become sloppy and impulsive, soon they begin to exercise their *license to hurt* one another.

"If you have no regard for the law," as the writer of Proverbs says, you are on a pathway to relational destruction. I pray that God will remind and discipline me to stay on the pathway to life, love, and joy—not destruction. How about you?

15

"Hunger..."

"Hunger has made us burn with fever until our skin is as hot as an oven." (Lamentations 5:10)

This is the first moon of the New Year, called by the Native Americans, the "Wolf Moon." They named all of the new moons of the year, and called the first new moon of January the "Wolf Moon" because in the still crisp air of the winter night the howling of the hungry wolves carried easily through the barren trees. Somehow I get the feeling that hearing hungry wolves howling not too far in the distance was not a comforting feeling. In fact, it probably was a reminder of the danger the tribal members might encounter in the woods when *hunger* in the form of a pack of powerful wolves was stalking their camp.

Hunger is dangerous, not only when it attacks from the outside in the form of a snarling wolf, but also when it attacks from the inside in physical, emotional, and spiritual manifestations. The biblical writer is right, hunger of any kind can make us "burn with fever," leaving us in such a vulnerable state that we are capable of doing things that might be considered *against our nature*. Physically hungry people are capable of stealing if they think it will fill their bellies. Emotionally hungry people are capable of striking out at others or getting lost in relational affairs if they think it will fill their hearts. Spiritually hungry people are capable of indulging in all sorts of destructive behaviors if they think it will fill their souls.

Alcoholics Anonymous helps lots of folks by using teaching acronyms. One such teaching tool is, *H.A.L.T.*, which stands for *Hungry, Angry, Lonely, and Tired*. The lesson is that all of us (not just those recovering from alcoholism) need to pay particular attention to when we are feeling, hungry, angry, lonely, or tired, because these emotions can cause us to "burn with fever" and become vulnerable to filling whatever hunger we might be feeling with our favorite destructive behaviors. Our hope for avoiding destruction comes in two ways. First, we need to fill our stomachs, hearts, and souls with a regular diet of healthy *food*. This will go a long way toward helping us avoid *uncontrollable hunger*. Second we need to pay careful attention to occasions when we might feel *hungry* so we don't become vulnerable to indulging ourselves with unhealthy *foods* or behaviors.

When we do feel particularly *hungry* we need to remove ourselves from potentially unhealthy environments and seek the help of our supportive friends and our God. I pray that God will help me stay on a healthy diet of his Word and Way so I avoid the destructive power of *uncontrollable hunger*. How about you?

16

"... It's poisoned! ..."

"The stew was poured out for the men to eat, but as soon as they tasted it they exclaimed to Elisha, 'It's poisoned!' ..." (II Kings 2:40)

I GUESS THIS FISH I found on a beach in Texas didn't get the message that there was poison in the pot in which he was swimming. In a way the fish re-

". . . It's poisoned! . . ."

minds me of the young woman who came to see me one day at my counseling office. She had a similar sort of *hollow* look about her as she explained that she had been an *exotic dancer*. She wondered out loud how she had missed the warning that there was emotional, spiritual *poison in the pot* where she was dancing.

She danced and danced until she literally danced her life away. Nothing remained but the shell of a young woman filled with remorse and shame. The poison in the pot in which she lived and danced hid its true intent behind the allure of false attraction and promise. She came to a pastoral counselor seeking healing and new life. She found what she needed in the grace of God in Christ. She found that God's love does forgive and renew.

In the book of II Kings from the Bible, the men alerted the prophet Elisha to the fact that the stew that was about to be served to the people contained deadly herbs. The prophet threw in some flour, served the stew, and no one was harmed. Once more, the power of God at work in the prophet brought transformation and life where only death was brewing.

God can heal and transform if we heed the warning and fall into divine love. I pray that God will help me hear the warning when I'm about to taste the *poison in a pot*, and help me serve the love of Christ to those who might have already tasted the *poison*. How about you?

17

"... you are worth much..."

"As for you, even the hairs of your head have all been counted. So do not be afraid; you are worth much more than many sparrows." (Matthew 10:30–31)

A PICTURE MAY BE *worth a thousand words*, but I'm not so sure this picture was worth the risk the young man was taking as he dangled out the window of his car to snap the shutter. Signs all over Yellowstone warned that this big

". . . you are worth much . . ."

grizzly and his relatives were extra hungry and extra mean because they had just emerged from hibernation. Beware!

Lent is a great time to stop and ask the question, "What is my life worth?" Is my life worth enough to cause me to stop unhealthy behaviors that risk mangling or ending it? Seems to me we can't tackle the question of what others' lives are worth to us until we first answer the question about our own life. Do we treat our life like we're worth something? Is my life worth anything, or is it worthless? Sometimes folks can reach a point where they think and act as though their life really is worthless. Maybe they've been hurt so much by others that they hear only the echoing of the scream, "You're worthless!"

Remember this—God has already weighed in on the question about your life. The Bible shares the story of how time and time again when God's people acted carelessly and suffered the ugly consequences of their own destructive decisions or were the victims of the hurtful behaviors launched upon them by others, God compassionately stepped in and offered loving re-recreation. Jesus was speaking about that compassion when he said we're worth so much that God would take the time to know us well enough to count the hairs on our head (or in some cases the hairs that used to be there.)

God wants to take the time to know you at the very core of your being. God doesn't want to throw you away. God wants to hold you closer. I pray that God will help me live my life like it's worth something. How about you?

18

"... not alone ..."

"The time is coming, and is already here, when all of you will be scattered, each of you to your own home, and I will be left all alone. But I am not really alone, because the Father is with me." (John 16:32)

"... *not alone* ..."

THE SIGN OUTSIDE THE hardware store read, "Chicks, ducks, and bunnies are in!" so I rolled into the parking lot and went inside with my camera. There I found two bins, one for ducks and one for chicks, with a little girl next to one holding and squeezing one of the chicks. The mother was giving the appropriate, "Now be careful," warnings, but I knew it was a real trial for the poor chick. (At least the chicks weren't dyed pastel colors like the ones I remember in the stores at Easter when I was a child.) This little duck in the picture with his head nestled against his sister's neck seems to be finding some sort of comfort in the midst of its trials. At least he's not alone in his trials!

There is probably little else we fear more than being totally, utterly alone, especially in times of trial and difficulty. Remember a time when you had a thought or feeling and believed you were the only one who experienced that? Remember what a relief you felt when someone disclosed their similar feeling and you discovered you weren't alone? We can feel alone in so many ways, but all the ways seem to lead to a similar sense of hurt, darkness, and even despair. Especially in times of greatest trial, we need to know we're not alone.

When Jesus was facing his time of greatest trial, he reminded his disciples that even though they would all be scared away from him, he would not be alone. God would be with him. That assurance gave Jesus the comfort and hope he needed to face his time of greatest suffering and pain. "Yet I am not alone, because the Father is with me."

As we Christians enter into our holiest of seasons in these coming days, we will celebrate and interpret the Easter event in many different ways. Too many times our *differences* have only served to separate and isolate us from one another. At its core God's Easter event in Jesus Christ boils down to one simple truth, *we are not alone—not now—not ever!* I pray that this Easter God will help me celebrate my oneness with other Christians and spread the Good News in Jesus Christ to others who so desperately need to hear—*we are not alone—not now—not ever!* How about you?

19

"... promise..."

"Even in my suffering I was comforted because your promise gave me life." (Psalm 119:50)

"... promise..."

WHILE WE WERE SUFFERING through a pretty oppressive winter, God's promise of fresh, new life was already at work. This little leaf was patiently waiting for the right combination of light and warmth to gently unfold itself and display the hope of a beautiful spring. Even as the snow was still falling and we were shivering and shoveling, God's promise of relief was present and waiting for God's moment to signal relief.

Suffering by its very nature is always difficult. Whether the suffering comes through physical or psychological distress, economic hardship, or relational crisis, the pain is always difficult, and even dangerous. Suffering can lead to despair, and despair can lead to the loss of life. One of the things that makes suffering bearable is promise—promise not only that suffering will end, but also promise that there will be new life on the other end of the suffering.

The end of suffering does not necessarily signal hope. The end of suffering can be simply numbness, not life. The drama unfolding this Holy Week reminds Christians that God knows our suffering completely. Jesus walked the path of deepest suffering as he endured denial and betrayal by his friends, physical abuse, and death. What got him through was promise—God's promise of life. It was the presence of that promise in the midst of the suffering that enabled Jesus to walk the path of suffering to be the Christ—our Christ—our promise.

God's promise is more than the end of suffering. God's promise is renewed and new life in response to our suffering. There is hope in life because we have God's promise even in the midst of our suffering. I pray that God will help me remember divine promise in the midst of suffering. How about you?

20

"... the water flows..."

"Then he gives a command, and the ice melts; he sends the wind, and the water flows. He gives his message to his people..." (Psalm 147:18-19)

". . . the water flows . . ."

A CLERGY RETREAT WITH our bishop has taken me to Blackwater Falls State Park in West Virginia, where the melted snow and ice fuel the falls and help the mountain flora and fauna begin to awaken from their winter slumber. God's command sparks life.

Who do you hear? Sometimes when I build a project I can almost hear my father telling me, "It needs one more nail." (We both subscribe to the principle that if one nail will hold it three will be even better—a principle I've come to later regret when I've had to dismantle some of my own projects.) What voice informs you? Whose instructions do you follow in your day-to-day life? There are many *voices* waiting to inform us. If we're not careful and deliberate about choosing which instructions to follow, we may find ourselves seduced by voices that beckon us for their own agenda.

God gives his message to his people, and his voice sparks life, not only in the mountains, but in our lives as well. It is critical that we pay careful attention to discern whose voice we are truly following. Whose voice do you hear when you listen? Spend time listening to God's Spirit for the message that will spark life for you. I pray that I will continue to hear and follow the message God gives through his Spirit. How about you?

21

"...we cannot deny it..."

"...we cannot deny it..."

"Everyone in Jerusalem knows that this extraordinary miracle has been performed by them, and we cannot deny it." (Acts 4:16)

I SAW THE FAMILY standing on the bridge over the small stream and heard one of them exclaim, "Look, there's a snake in the water." Joining them on the bridge I discovered, sure enough, there was a snake periodically poking its head above the water and changing positions in between. Then someone pointed out the frog a few feet away from the snake and noted that the snake was trying to sneak up on the unsuspecting frog. I readied my camera to catch *the catch*. Just then, the family decided to move on. One little girl lagged behind long enough to throw a stick in the water and say, "I don't want the frog to be eaten for dinner." In a flash, both predator and prey disappeared. I'm sure the little girl slept a little better that evening knowing the snake didn't eat the frog (at least not while she was around).

Sometimes denial that keeps certain things out of our active consciousness serves a healthy purpose. Most of us probably get into our cars each day without contemplating the hundreds of deaths that occur from auto accidents that very same day. I would call that a form of denial. Our awareness of auto tragedies stays buried deeply enough in our consciousness to allow us to travel comfortably in our cars and deny that anything bad will happen to us. Too much awareness of the dangers could make us anxious enough that we might be more susceptible to getting our selves and others into auto accidents. Sometimes denial works for our good.

Many times we use denial in an unhealthy way. We attempt to deny things that might challenge us to look at ourselves and recognize the need for change. The power of God's love at work in Jesus and later in his disciples often challenged folks to change hurtful ways of relating to one another. Sometimes the presence of God's love evoked efforts to deny the call to change. Such was the case in the story from Acts when God's love worked through Peter to heal a lame beggar and the miracle caused the ruling Council to want to deny it. The Council desperately wanted to avoid the change that God's love in Christ was demanding of them. They wanted to deny the miracle but knew that would bring even more trouble. "Everyone in Jerusalem knows that this extraordinary miracle has been performed by them, and we cannot deny it."

When we deny the reality that we may be doing something harmful to our selves or others the result is always the same. The hurt grows like an invasive cancer until it squeezes the life from the individual or relationship. God's love in Christ challenges us to change hurtful behaviors. Denial will only make things worse. I pray that God will challenge me with his love and strengthen me to avoid the temptation to hide in denial. How about you?

22

". . . watch where you are going . . ."

"Those who are good travel a road that avoids evil; so watch where you are going—it may save your life." (Proverbs 16:17)

PATTI SPOTTED THE YOUNG groundhog as he made his way along the riverbank, surprisingly far away from any burrow in sight. He seemed like he was intently focused on some sort of mission as he scurried along. Maybe

Wednesday Wonderings

that's why he failed to take into account that his chosen path would take him past a pair of geese sunning their twelve goslings by the water's edge. However, I don't think that's a mistake this groundhog will make a second time. His choice of paths gave him quite a scare and might have cost him more had he not skedaddled on his way.

Sometimes we find ourselves in one of life's *ditches* moaning, groaning and wondering how we wound up in such a predicament. Yet often, life is not as complicated as we like to make it seem. If we choose roads that take us down or near the curves of unhealthy living (or *sin* as we call it) then it shouldn't be a surprise when we find ourselves in the *ditch*, or like that groundhog, *getting our tail nipped.*

Jesus invited us to receive his love, learn from his love, and follow his way (or road). His road is the one with the sign marking the way that says, "Love one another." All other roads lead the wrong way. Choosing the right road makes a very real difference in our lives, "so watch where you're going—it may save your life." I pray that God will help me choose the right road. How about you?

23

"... satisfied ..."

"My soul will feast and be satisfied, and I will sing glad songs of praise to you." (Psalm 63:5)

LATELY I'VE BEEN LEARNING a lot from butterflies. Last year as I began to take more photographs I found myself chasing a lot of butterflies. I must have looked pretty crazy trying to keep up with the magnificent creatures as they flitted erratically from blossom to blossom. Finally, after observing them long enough and being frustrated with a lot of blurred shots of butterflies on the move, I got the lesson they were trying to convey (sort of like a "duh" moment as the teens would say). I learned that if I wanted a good butterfly photo I had to wait for one of the critters to find just the right flower. When they found it they would cling to the blossom, unfurl their tongue, and drink deeply of the nectar—posing for several moments and allowing me to take several decent photos. When the butterfly finds the nectar it needs, the critter stops its furious flittering and drinks deeply until it is satisfied.

Finding God, or rather accepting the love of God that finds us, is only the first step of the journey. I see too many folks today *accepting the Lord* and then flittering away. They don't give themselves the opportunity to stay connected and grow in their awareness of God's love, and be transformed by God's love so they can truly share God's love with others. Instead, they have a more momentary encounter with God and then return to the same life as before, filled with endless distractions and fruitless searches for fulfillment.

If we want our souls to be satisfied like the psalmist, we must stop our own frenzied flittering and drink deeply from the water of life that only God can offer. As we travel along our way, we must continue to make the time to cling to God, to drink from the well of God's presence, and feel satisfied by the peace that comes from taking God in more and more along the way. There's no shortcut to this satisfaction. We have to spend more time focusing on God each day in whatever way is meaningful for each of us. I want my soul to be satisfied, so I pray that God will help me when I succumb to fruitless, frenzied, flittering. How about you?

24

"... upside down."

"They turn everything upside down." (Isaiah 29:16)

WERE IT NOT FOR the ripple in the water's surface you might look at the picture and assume my camera was pointed up at the sky instead of down at the water. My camera might have turned your world upside down and fooled you into believing that you were looking at the sky instead of the sky reflecting on the water. (I purposely had my wife, Patti make the ripple so you wouldn't be fooled.)

I don't mind being fooled as part of a joke but I really, really dislike being fooled in a serious situation. I remember more than once when I was a young, inexperienced pastor being told stories by individuals only later to find I had been fooled. Being fooled makes me feel angry, hurt, disappointed, weak, and much more wary about trusting the next time. Unfortunately it's not that difficult to deceive us, to get us to believe that down is up and up is down.

Deceit can sneak up on us before we know it. Persons with power and position can easily get us to believe their version of reality when we are manipulated by our desires for everything from safety and certainty to lust and greed. We can even learn to deceive our very own selves if we allow our wants to distract us from our focus—healthy relationship with God and one another.

Isaiah indicted God's people by accusing them, saying, "They turn everything upside down." He was speaking to a people who had neglected the practice of their faith. Once they began to neglect the study of God's word and practice of the covenant they became easy prey for their own delusions and the manipulation of others. They began to believe down was up and up was down. Right was wrong and wrong was right. They began to believe that their *wants* were more important than God's way and manipulated *reality* to reflect their wants. The result was not very pretty for them, nor is it for us when we do the same.

It's pretty painful when we come to the awareness that our world has been turned upside down by the deceitfulness of our selves and others. I give thanks to God that I can turn to God and find in the love of Christ forgiveness, healing, and the help to practice a faith in God that will inform and not deceive. How about you?

25

"... worms ..."

"As Moses had commanded, they kept what was left until the next day; it did not spoil or get worms in it." (Exodus 16:24)

NOT YET, BUT SOON ... worms, that is. The flies were busily laying their eggs in the carcass of the bird I found in the church parking lot. In not too long a time the eggs will hatch into maggots (worms), the maggots will eat and help decompose the bird carcass, then the maggots will become flies and so on and so on and so on . . . or at least that's the way the process is supposed to work.

As the Israelites followed Moses out of Egypt and began their trek through the desert their anxiety was sky high. How would they eat, how would they live, where would they find water, where would they go? The questions poured endlessly from their lips as they struggled with their vulnerability and anxiety. That's also why when the manna God sent to sustain them began to appear in the mornings, they disobeyed the first day, collected more than the amount needed for the day as they were directed, and wound up with maggot-infested leftover manna. Their anxiety about the future won out over listening to and following God's guidance. After that, it must have been especially tough for the Israelites when they got to the sixth day and Moses told them to collect enough manna for two days (so they wouldn't work on the Sabbath).

Their reasoning told them to pay attention to the lesson they'd already learned—that leftover manna spoils and grows maggots. "As Moses had commanded, they kept what was left until the next day; it did not spoil or get worms in it." Let's see, they got maggots when they anticipated none, and none when they anticipated maggots. Hmm, finally, they learned that following God's message through Moses meant sometimes acting counter to how the *reasonable* action might direct them.

God's message for life as spoken and demonstrated by Jesus then continually whispered by the Holy Spirit ("Love the Lord your God with all your heart and soul and mind, and your neighbor as yourself") sometimes trumps lessons learned from reason and may leave us with unanticipated outcomes. God's Spirit may lead us in ways of seemingly irrational loving. I recently read that the exaltation of the rights of individuals above all else seems to be becoming more the norm in our country today. Given that premise, God's whispering to our souls to, "love our neighbors as ourselves," by giving of our selves to others, might seem very unreasonable and irrational.

Maggots or no maggots, hmm, let me see . . . O God, I pray that your Spirit will continue to whisper your message of life in my soul, and that I will have the courage to listen and follow, even when the *reasoning of the day* would have me go another direction. How about you?

26

"... boldly and without hindrance..."

"He preached about the Kingdom of God and taught about the Lord Jesus Christ, speaking with all boldness and freedom." (Acts 28:31)

"Just a little more and this ball will be ours!!!!" *Amen!!* They've been through at least ten of those balls over the course of a couple of years.

Somehow Tinker Bell and Peter Pan do throw themselves into the chase with such boldness and abandon that they manage to get their teeth into it, and . . . *Pop!!!*

Paul was a man who responded to God's call on his life by offering the good news of God's love in Christ to the world. Although several books in the Bible are attributed to him, the book of Acts contains narratives about him. The writer of Acts ends his account of Paul's life with the scripture quoted above. The last words written about Paul say that he went about his work for the Lord with all boldness and freedom. How would it feel to have that written as the last word about your life?

We need some boldness and freedom today. As Christians we, too, need to *boldly go* into a world suffering from fear, anxiety, anger, and greed. We need to boldly proclaim and offer the peace, love, and wholeness we find in Christ. It's no time for timidity. Hate mongers are busily plying their trade, screaming their anthems louder and louder. This is no time for half-hearted efforts by God's people. I pray that God will give me the energy to boldly live and share the peace of Christ! How about you?

27

"... hold on to what is good."

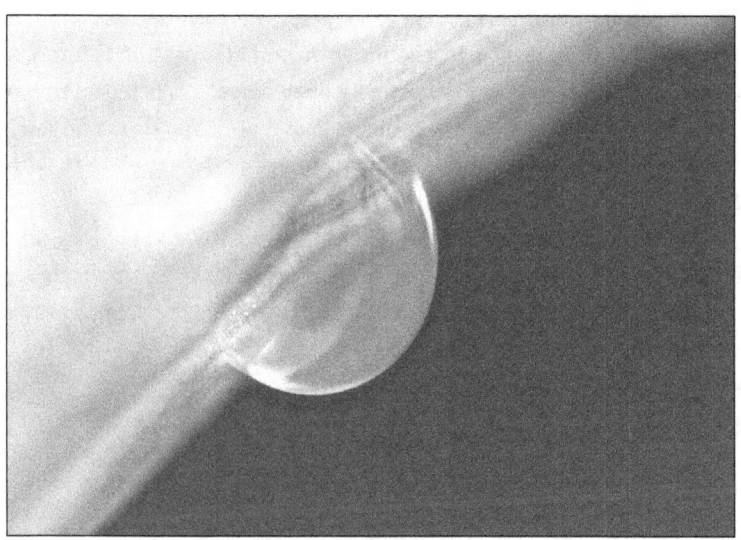

"Love must be completely sincere. Hate what is evil, hold on to what is good." (Romans 12:9)

A DROPLET OF WATER holds on or *clings* to the bottom of a flower petal. *Wow*, what a miracle! Some powerful force must be at work to enable such a bond. When the force weakens, the water no longer clings, and falls to the ground with a *splat*. A miracle becomes an ordinary *splat*. I looked up the definition of "cling," and found that "to cling" means, "to hold on tightly," or, "to remain very close," or, "to remain persistently or stubbornly faithful to something."

I like that. I think we need more persistent, stubborn faithfulness today. "No matter what happens, I'm not letting go!" That's what I want to hear when I'm dangling over the rail of some difficult situation. I want to know that someone loves me sincerely enough that they're clinging to me—persistently, stubbornly, faithfully holding on to me. I hear that loud and clear from God. I also need to hear it from those around who say they love me. If that's what I need then I suspect it's what others need as well.

I'm not talking about someone being *too clingy*. That's an unhealthy situation where one person becomes overly dependent on another and loses their sense of self and direction. I'm talking about the kind of clinging that brings health to relationships, a passionate *holding on* instead of a lackadaisical, ho-hum sort of co-existence. The Apostle Paul knew that in matters of faith and the love that flows from faith, passion is important. Nothing can be lackadaisical! That's why he exhorted his listeners to have a sincere love for God and one another, a love that demands action—a love that compels the person to move away from evil and cling to good with all of their might.

If we fail to love passionately, clinging to what we know is good and who is good for us, we become just another splat! It's not complicated, and it's not pretty. Without sincere love that clings, we fall and splat! I pray that God will teach me to cling! How about you?

28

"... my plans have failed ..."

"My days have passed; my plans have failed; my hope is gone." (Job 17:11)

I WAS PROFOUNDLY STRUCK by what seemed like the lingering pain and suffering seeping from the walls as I walked the hallways of the abandoned

Wednesday Wonderings

Transallegheny Lunatic Asylum (better known to many in more recent years as the old Weston State Hospital). As I stared out this shattered window it made me particularly mindful of those who stood at the windows of their rooms in the asylum for much of their lives, watching the world pass them by. For many of them it was the feeling that, "My days have passed; my plans have failed; my hope is gone" that brought them to the asylum.

Their depression and despair became their prison before they ever entered the asylum. When plans are shattered, even very important plans, most of us experience hurt, frustration, maybe even grief, but eventually find our way through to making new plans. Yet there are those suffering from illnesses like depression who experience shattered plans much more intensely. They're not trying to *be dramatic* or to get us to *feel sorry for them*.

The illness called, *depression* makes the disappointment feel so intense inside that it can seem like not only have plans been shattered but also, hope. If there are is no hope, then maybe there is no future. If we are to help those who suffer from these dreaded illnesses like depression, we must first understand that their experience on the inside is not the same as our own. Even if we shared the same shattered plans, I might experience *hurt* while my friend suffering from depression might experience *Hurt!* Recognizing this difference will help me avoid the pitfalls of judging my friend that tend to close doors leading toward healing.

When I hurt I count on the restorative love of God to heal and guide. I want that for all. I pray that God will help me point others in the same direction, not hinder them with judgment. How about you?

29

"... relief ..."

"The Lord will give the people of Israel relief from their pain and suffering..." (Isaiah 14:3)

PATTI AND I VISITED the coastal area of Maine last week in the midst of a heat wave with temperatures in the nineties. Relief is so critical in our lives—relief from our own pain and suffering, relief from the pain and suffering of others, relief from our labor, and even relief from the oppressive heat that suffocated the eastern part of our country last week. (Thought I'd try to offer some relief with a photo from a winter's visit to Maine instead of one from the ninety-eight degree heat we experienced.)

Relief is one of many gifts from God. Sometimes relief comes after much anticipation, sometimes it surprises us. Regardless of how and when it arrives, relief is something to be welcomed and cherished. Yet, there are times when we may find it almost difficult to celebrate relief. When loved ones end their long struggles with illness and finally leave us to join God's heavenly celebration, sometimes it's difficult for those left behind to relish the relief they feel from daily trips to the hospital and agonizing hours by the bedside. After all, why should I deserve relief when my loved one just died? It's difficult to feel relief when others still suffer. Yet relief is truly a gift from God. Like all gifts from God, relief is not just for me. Even though it is the relief that I experience, the relief renews and prepares me to be in further service for others.

Do you need relief from something? It's more than just okay to pray for relief. It's a necessity. I pray that God will give me the gift of relief when needed so I might better continue to serve. How about you?

30

"... made completely new ..."

"So get rid of your old self, which made you live as you used to—the old self that was being destroyed by its deceitful desires. Your hearts and minds must be made completely new, and you must put on the new self, which is created in God's likeness and reveals itself in the true life that is upright and holy." (Ephesians 4:22-24)

Wednesday Wonderings

I'VE SEEN A HUMMINGBIRD—AND I've seen a moth—but I'd never seen such a thing as a hummingbird moth until this week when one showed up at the butterfly bush in our front yard. I was spellbound. I took the picture without knowing what the creature was until a friend helped me identify it. I am totally in awe of the way God manages to surprise me. I chased that moth around the bush for several minutes.

Do you remember the excitement of finding or experiencing something new? The *new* can invite us into a transformational moment of joy and hope. What a gift God gives us when we are invited to experience the newness of life. It is also a gift to be invited into the experience of being, "made completely new," as the scripture says.

We get stuck in hurtful places for lots of different reasons. Sometimes we get stuck because of hurt that is done to us by others. Sometimes we get stuck because of some sort of illness like depression. Sometimes we get stuck because we fall victim to *bad habits* that fool us into believing they offer sustenance and hope. Regardless of how we get stuck, God makes it clear that divine love can point us toward something new and transforming so we're no longer stuck, but rather, being, "made completely new." God's love in Christ is waiting to point us toward hope.

We've all heard of the necessity of an *attitude adjustment*. New actions, new ideas, new hopes and dreams often flow from such an *adjustment*. Without the *adjustment* we remain stuck—regardless of how we got there. God's love is often a correcting force to remind us of the need for *adjustment* if we are to experience the new life offered. I pray that God will continue to make me completely new. How about you?

31

"... unfailing love..."

"Yet hope returns when I remember this one thing: The Lord's unfailing love and mercy still continue, fresh as the morning, as sure as the sunrise." (Lamentations 3:21-23)

Wednesday Wonderings

Okay, you're right—it's either the north end of a bird flying south or the south end of a bird flying north. Take your pick. I didn't crop the head out of the picture. I just missed the head altogether when I took the photo. I've learned with my new incarnation in photography that in order to get *the perfect shot* I usually mess up several others. Thank goodness for digital cameras. If I were still using film the cost of so many botched photos would end my photographic meanderings and you'd not be seeing much of *Wednesday Wonderings*.

I've seen a lot of dramas on TV and movies where the hero proclaims, "Failure is not an option." I find that failure is always an option. I don't want to fail, I don't like to fail, I hope I don't fail, I do everything within my power not to fail, but failure is an option and a reality. I have failed in the past and will fail in the future. I can either choose to live in the fear of failure or the hope of possibilities.

I choose hope and possibilities knowing that failure may be a lesson along the way, but joy is the reward of the journey. My choice is possible because of one thing and one thing alone. I know that when I do fail, there is something else that does not fail—God's love for me. I will fail, but God will forgive, instruct, redeem, and renew. The experience of that never-failing love is what gives me the courage to choose a path of hope and possibilities over fear of failure and stagnation.

We call this never-failing love, *grace*. I give thanks for God's grace when I fail and pray for divine help to extend that grace to others in their failings. How about you?

32

"... in constant pain..."

"I am about to fall and am in constant pain." (Psalms 38:17)

OUCH! I REMEMBER AS a young boy wandering through the woods with my buddies, stumbling upon a barbed wire fence, and trying to figure out if we should go over, under, or through it. (Be real—the thought rarely crossed our minds that *none of the above* and *stay out* were the correct choices. We were explorers!) Inevitably, one of us would get hung up on the fence and have to explain the torn shirt or pants to mom. Ouch!

The barbed wire fence in the picture is meant for one purpose—to send a painful message to a cow bumping against it, a message that screams, "Back off, stay inside the pasture where it's safe. Don't go out on the road and pretend you're a deer waiting to be hit by a passing car." The painful message from the barbed wire sends an important message to the cow that just might save its life (at least until it reaches the slaughterhouse.)

Much of the time pain serves a similar purpose in our lives. The presence of pain alerts us to something that might not be quite right, either, physically, emotionally, or spiritually. Although it *hurts*, physical pain can save our lives. It can make us aware of something malfunctioning inside our body that needs attention before more damage is created. Emotional and spiritual pain can do the same, confronting us with hurtful decisions we might be making or situations in which we might be living.

In a sense, pain is a call to change, a call that hopefully can be heard and heeded. Sometimes when physical pain is ignored we hear the stories like undetected cancers and tumors getting a head start on their hosts. When emotional and spiritual pain is ignored it might well be turned into a destructive force directed toward one's own self or others.

Pain must be heard before anything else can happen. The psalmist was in deep, unrelenting pain when he wrote, "I am about to fall and am in constant pain." He screamed his pain to God with the confidence he would be heard. Some pain may be overwhelming and seemingly endless, defying the efforts of professionals and others to find help and healing. Even then, it can be worse. It can be worse if we feel no one wants to hear our pain, in other words, no one cares if we hurt.

Even when we feel helpless in the face of the pain of others, it's critical that they know we're listening to their pain. We hear them. We're with them. We care. I pray that God will help me listen to pain that calls me to change, and pain that calls me to care. How about you?

33

"... why worry..."

"Look at the crows: they don't plant seeds or gather a harvest; they don't have storage rooms or barns; God feeds them! You are worth so much more than birds!" (Luke 12:24–25)

ON SUNDAY EVENING I spotted the bug, recently stuck in the spider's web but still alive and kicking, struggling to free itself from its pending doom.

Wednesday Wonderings

By the next afternoon, the bug was hardly recognizable as it hung neatly wrapped beside a decapitated grasshopper in the spider's meat locker.

Somehow I take comfort knowing that I am part of my God's plan that is so amazing that even spiders have meat lockers. As soon as I mention *God's plan* I know I've stepped into dangerous territory. Some might ask, "Are you saying that God plans for spiders to have food and plans for children to starve?" *No, I do not think that child abuse, starvation, rape, murder, or any other kind of violence or suffering is part of God's plan.* I do not know why some are hurt and suffer while others prosper. I plan to ask God all about that someday. However, when I find myself starting to worry about my own difficulties or the difficulties of others it does help me when I remember something like the spider's meat locker, or the "crows" as the writer of the Gospel of Luke would say. It helps me to know that all of us are part of something much bigger than ourselves, something so miraculous, something planned and made by the one who knows me in every detail.

Pain and suffering threaten us with spiritual extinction. They try to make us believe that we only have two choices: we either have to embrace the notion that God plans hurtful things to happen, or we must run away from that thought and instead, believe there is no plan—there is no God, and thus no hope. I've seen too many *spiders' meat lockers* and other such stuff to believe there is nothing. I pray that when I start to worry God will remind me of spider's meat lockers. How about you?

34

"... keep watch with me..."

"Grief and anguish came over him, and he said to them, 'The sorrow in my heart is so great that it almost crushes me. Stay here and keep watch with me.'" (Matthew 26:37–38)

Wednesday Wonderings

Ever have one of those days—weeks—months—years—one where everything seemed so overwhelming that you wanted to stay in the bed or go back to bed and just pull the covers up over your head? (At least this guy in the picture could have gone back to his bed instead of mine). Know what I mean? Of course you do. We've all had times in our lives when we've felt overwhelmed—maybe so overwhelmed that even the light at the end of the tunnel seemed too distant with just too many obstacles between us and the freedom of the tunnel entrance. What we needed was the light for just the next step.

To be overwhelmed is to feel as though the future is just one big leap across the river with no stepping-stones between you and the other side. Lacking stones to make even the smallest step and progress, why bother to even try. "You'll never make it, no one could make such a leap across the entire river," the overwhelmed mind tells it's captive. "Just go back to bed and pull the covers tighter around your head."

There are many life experiences that can lead us to that trap of being overwhelmed. Tragedies and crises can bring such intense sorrow and sadness that we may feel temporarily overwhelmed. Illnesses like depression can also leave us feeling overwhelmed. Sometimes when we're not feeling overwhelmed it's hard for us to imagine why folks look like they're *giving up*, or *not trying*. We see the stepping-stones in the river, why don't they see them? The state of being overwhelmed robs the individual of the ability to take large challenges and break them into smaller, manageable pieces. Life becomes all or nothing. The river is too wide to jump, so why bother to try.

The Bible says that even Jesus became overwhelmed by sorrow as he contemplated the future hours of his life leading up to his death. Yet he did two important things. First, he asked his friends to help him, and second, he asked God to help him. Often when we feel overwhelmed we need others to shine God's light of hope so we can see just the next step. We need help breaking down those seemingly impossible life moments into smaller manageable experiences. Sometimes that help comes from friends and sometimes it also needs to come from professionals. I pray that when I feel overwhelmed God will send me the light for the next step, and help me hold the light for others. How about you?

35

"... helped ..."

"But to this very day I have been helped by God . . ." (Acts 26:22)

I SPOTTED HIM ON the way to the church picnic and had to stop. The Billy goat and his buddies really didn't seem too bothered by his dilemma. When

Wednesday Wonderings

I walked to the fence to take the picture he made his way over and seemed to want help (or maybe, no probably, food).

Anyway, I reached over the fence, removed his *crown*, and watched while he and his buddies proceeded to eat it. The weed was wrapped around his horns pretty tightly so I doubt he would have been able to remove it by himself—and I doubt he would have had the patience to stand still long enough for his friends to eat the weed while it still entangled him. This Billy needed help.

Sometimes I think we live in a culture that seems tipped too much toward rugged individualism. Don't get me wrong, it's certainly important that we work hard to do our best and succeed at our goals. A stubborn *git 'er done* (by myself) attitude is necessary at times. However, too often I watch as folks needlessly suffer because they're afraid to ask for help. What's so scary about asking for help? If I ask for help does it imply I'm weak, does it mean I lack character? No, the truth of the matter is that we all have limits and all find ourselves at times in need of help.

We may not realize it, but we all "have been helped by God . . . " None of us could live without the sustaining, life-giving power of God at work in all of life and in each of our individual lives. Without God's ever present help there would be no life. The more we allow ourselves to acknowledge God's help, appreciate God's help, and celebrate God's help the more we will be able to accomplish our goals in harmony with God's goals. It also means that when we come upon our limitations we will be more comfortable asking for more help from God and one another.

I am grateful for God's help and pray that nothing like fear, stubbornness, or anything else will get in the way of my asking for God's help or your help when I'm in need. How about you?

36

"The Lord will make sure . . ."

". . . The Lord will make sure that you and I, and your descendants and mine, will forever keep the sacred promise we have made to each other." (I Samuel 20:42)

"The Lord will make sure . . ."

BRIDGE CLOSED! THAT'S A sign that can bring tragedy and heart ache to any community. Long-standing relationships can become strained and compromised when the *bridge* is out. I grew up until I was eight years old on the Kentucky side of the Tug River. If all the bridges had closed we would have been deprived of many of our needs from *town* on the West Virginia side.

A *bridge closing* is one of the most dangerous things for any relationship. When communication breaks down and two parties cease talking to one another the result is often catastrophic. When two parties refuse to talk with each other they begin to objectify the other, seeing them less of a human and more of an *it*. Once a *person* becomes an *it*, there's not too long a time before *it* becomes a *target*. Then *targets* become fair game for fear, hatred, and lots of other ugly feelings.

In the Old Testament Jonathan pledges that although his father, King Saul, hates David enough to want to kill him, Jonathan will always have peace with David because the Lord will be the bridge between them. God's love and mercy can serve as the bridge between us, calling us back to talking with one another when our failings threaten human relationships. God's love calls us to talk—to relate as human to human. God's love can be the bridge between us—the bridge that is never closed. I pray that God will always show me the bridge. How about you?

37

"He leads the humble..."

**"He leads the humble in the right way and teaches them his will."
(Psalms 24:9)**

I REMEMBER DRIVING THROUGH the country in a rural area and coming upon a house with a fence encircling the property. Next to the gate in the fence was a sign that read, "Guard dog can reach this gate in 4 seconds. Can You?" The sign was meant to conjure up a moment of humility for the would-be thief, reminding the thief that even with all their cunning and experience, their plans might fail simply because the guard dog most likely could beat them in a sprint. Fearing the business end of the dog, the thief (hopefully) would be humbled and deterred.

I couldn't help wondering if a similar sign was posted on my hummingbird feeder warning the impatient bird about the business end of the bee gathering sugar water from the feeder. Humility is important because it makes us teachable. Without humility, without an awareness of our limits, we simply are not very teachable and are therefore much more likely to meet the business end of something with a *bite* or a *sting*. Humility also invites us to respect the *teacher*, some other who has what we lack but need. Humility invites us into relationship, because at it's very essence it reminds us that we are not alone and cannot survive alone.

Humility is not *bad*. It is not shameful. On the contrary, it points us to the way out of our shame by reminding us to give thanks to God, the one who forgives and renews by continuing to teach us his way. I pray that God will call me to humility and teach me what is right, his way. How about you?

38

"... swords into plows ..."

"... They will hammer their swords into plows and their spears into pruning knives. Nations will never again go to war; never prepare for battle again." (Micah 4:3)

". . . swords into plows . . ."

LAST WEEKEND OUR COMMUNITY celebrated an annual festival, with the festivities on Saturday evening punctuated by a fantastic fireworks display. In fact, it was so phenomenal I heard folks invoking the "D" word as they disappeared into the night saying, "Those fireworks were even better than Disney!" I found myself wondering about all that gunpowder rolled tightly together with other chemicals to explode in fantastic arrays of colored lights and sound. Then I thought about the verse from Micah, "They will hammer their swords into plows . . ." When gunpowder is being exploded in fireworks it means it's not being exploded in bombs—swords into plowshares. Resources must be used for peace, not war.

In personal relationships (and international affairs for that matter) the mere absence of conflict is not peace. If the absence of conflict simply means rusty swords are hung on the wall, the swords are available at moment's notice for hacking and slashing. In order for peace to truly exist in a relationship the parties must not only cease fighting, they must also agree to find new ways of relating and disagreeing that preclude *fighting*. They must actively beat their swords into plowshares so the swords are not hanging on the walls waiting for the next disagreement to turn into a *fight*. As the prophet Micah says, "Nations will never again go to war . . ."

Instead of simply temporarily ending the *armed conflict* the individuals must learn and practice with great discipline ways of relating that are respectful and compassionate. The parties must use their emotional resources for loving, not fighting. They must diligently learn and practice the ways of peace, not war. Unfortunately, I've seen far too many relationships and marriages end because disagreements turned into fights, and fights turned into irreconcilable wars. Ways of peace were not diligently practiced in the relationships and the paths to fighting were just too worn and well traveled. In those homes, rusty swords hung over the mantle as reminders of the willingness to *fight*.

Healthy relationships are evidenced by the absence of swords over the mantle and instead, rust-free plows in the barns—plows that have been busy sowing the seeds of peace. I pray that God will teach me the ways of peace, and help me sow its seeds wherever possible. How about you?

39

"... disappears..."

"... what am I going to do with you? Your love for me disappears as quickly as morning mist; it is like dew that vanishes early in the day. What I want from you is plain and clear: I want your constant love..." (Hosea 6:4-6)

"... disappears..."

I WAS ALREADY RUNNING late for a morning meeting when I passed the low-lying mist over the blooming pasture. "Wow, what a great a picture," I thought. "I'll get it on my way back." I barely finished the thought before reminding myself, "Wait a minute, the picture you want won't be there when you return. The mist will be gone." I turned around, stopped the car, and got the picture. Like morning mist, some things don't last. Love shouldn't be one of them.

"Do you still love me?" Ever been asked that question? If you have, then you know it can be rather startling. "What do you mean, do I still love you? Of course I still love you. Can't you tell?" Obviously, the answer is, "no," or the question would not have been asked. Unfortunately we don't always do a great job of communicating our love for one another over the long haul. We get lazy and sloppy. We forget that to truly love another is to cherish each other.

To cherish another means to constantly move caring energy toward them. Of course, the intensity of that loving energy will ebb and flow, but it better not drop to the point that our partner wonders, "Do you still love me?" When loving energy drops to that level, it opens the door for other issues and conflicts that begin to destroy the relationship.

I'm one who is convinced that most relationships that fail do so because folks get sloppy and lazy with one another. The relationships don't fail because the couples first encounter huge irreconcilable problems. The sloppiness and laziness comes first. They're loving energy begins to wane and eventually, "disappears as quickly as morning mist."

God's cry to the people of Israel through the prophet Hosea is the same as our cry to one another, "I want your constant love." Anything less means love will begin to fade like a morning mist. If someone is worth loving, then they're worth loving constantly. That's certainly God's message about how we're divinely loved—constantly! I pray that God will remind me when my love is anything less than *constant*. How about you?

40

"... I was a stranger..."

"... I was a stranger and you received me in your homes..." (Matthew 25:35)

I'M GROWING RATHER FOND of these fellows. On a hot sunny day they pause for several moments, almost posing for my camera. This damselfly looks strange and quite intimidating. Although they're not harmful to humans, that *whatchamacallit* thing on the end at least looks like it could deliver quite a sting—but it doesn't. As a matter of fact these damselflies are not only safe, they also consume many of the critters like flies and mosquitoes that irritate us. I've gotten to know these damselflies so I'm no longer concerned that one might sting me. We're no longer *strangers*!

There are strangers among us. They may not necessarily be from a different neighborhood, state, or country. The strangers are more often somehow *different* from us in other ways so we call them *strange* and treat them like strangers. All sorts of rumors and myths grow around *them*. We think they're *different* and *strange* so they must be dangerous. I've learned over the years that when we get to know the *stranger* we generally start to realize that they're more like us than unlike us. Strangers who once were labeled as *one of them* are transformed into *one of us* when we risk getting to know each other and welcome *them* into our lives and our hearts.

Jesus knew the transforming power of love to bind us together when fear and hate would keep us strangers. He said, "I was a stranger and you received me in your homes . . ." I pray that God's love will always challenge me to receive the stranger. How about you?

41

"... minds ready for action..."

". . . minds ready for action . . ."

"So then, have your minds ready for action. Keep alert . . . Be obedient to God, and do not allow your lives to be shaped by those desires you had when you were still ignorant. Instead, be holy in all that you do . . ." (I Peter 1: 13-15)

Parent: "So why did you do this?"
  Child: "Everyone else was doing it!"
  Parent: "If everyone else was jumping off a cliff would you jump too?"
  I'm not an expert on ants, but apparently there are situations where the little boy and girl ants would answer that parental question with, "Yes." One day near the end of summer I looked at my hummingbird feeder only to discover that suddenly hundreds and hundreds of ants had unwittingly followed one another *right over the cliff*. In this case the *cliff* was the edge of my feeder, with a sugar-watery death awaiting them inside.

Our parents tried to warn us about *following*—or more likely, *following without thinking*. They wanted us to beware the tendency of taking the easy road, blindly following without using our brains and the important knowledge we had been given to sort our way through the many difficult challenges of life. There are many who would like for us to forget the warnings of our parents as well as the warning of the writer of I Peter in the New Testament.

Sometimes it seems likes the *band wagons* are circled around us with each of their leaders cajoling us to climb aboard. "You don't have to think, you don't have to wonder, and you don't have to worry. Just climb on my wagon and everything will be okie-dokie!" *Band Wagon Leaders* know how to prey upon our vulnerabilities. They know how to hit us where it *hurts*—especially triggering those feelings the writer of I Peter had in mind when he said, "do not allow your lives to be shaped by those desires you had when you were still ignorant."

Those *desires* are often reflections of our anxiety and emerge as the desire to be safe, the desire to be liked, the desire to belong, the desire to be happy, etc. When we forget what we've learned—that our deepest desire is to know peace, a peace that is available from God through all times and all things, we will allow ourselves to turn off our *thinking* and blindly climb aboard the most attractive *bandwagon*. I Peter's writer is right in saying we are no longer ignorant. Jesus reminded us that the way to holiness (and peace) is "to love the Lord with all our heart and soul and mind and strength, and our neighbor as our self."

When faced with struggles of life that demand decisions, I pray that God will give me the courage resist the temptation to jump on a bandwagon, and instead, use the tools and knowledge God has given me to find my way and "be holy." How about you?

42

"... different gifts ..."

"So we are to use our different gifts in accordance with the grace that God has given us ..." (Romans 12:6)

Wednesday Wonderings

The wood chips were flying yesterday as my neighbor and resident chain saw carver launched into another one of his creations. I am always amazed how artists can see something hidden in their medium and help it come to life. I saw a block of wood. My neighbor saw the Ohio State University mascot and helped him escape from the block.

When I was a young teen still living at home and contemplating my future my mother would sometimes ask me two annoying questions. (Well, at least at the time they seemed annoying. Now I realize they were and still remain critical questions for all of us to ask our selves.) The first question was, "What gifts has God given you?" The second question was, "How is God calling you to use those gifts?" See what I mean? They were *annoying* to a teen because they made me have to really think and wrestle. It felt like my teen brain already hurt from too much thinking.

Now I know how critical the questions were and still are today. God sees in us the divine gifts that have been given, and calls them forth from us. If we listen, ask, and act we may discover things about our selves we never imagined possible. We may find our selves on some path we never imagined. We may find our selves engaged in God's service in ways we never imagined. "So we are to use our different gifts in accordance with the grace that God has given us." Amen! I believe those gifts are waiting for us to use them in the service of God's kingdom. I pray that God will always help me continue to ask my mother's two *annoying* questions and act on the answers that are revealed. How about you?

43

"When I look at the sky . . ."

"When I look at the sky, which you have made, at the moon and the stars, which you set in their places—what are human beings, that you think of them; mere mortals, that you care for them? Yet you made them inferior only to yourself; you crowned them with glory and honor." (Psalms 8:3-5)

Wednesday Wonderings

"WHEN I LOOK AT . . ." (or as others translations say, "consider"). That's a vital statement! Believe it or not I think it all begins with taking the time to "look at," to "consider," or "wonder." (Why else do you think *Wednesday Wonderings* is so important for me?) It's when we stop to *consider* that our spiritual journey and our life receive a blessing beyond belief.

Today we live in a world where we are almost constantly *entertained* with information and amusement. The next time you're in a public place with others waiting for something, notice the number of folks who are using electronic devices to catch up on messages, play games, etc. Our electronic connections are great at times, but also run the risk of filling our every waking moment and leaving very little opportunity for simply *considering*.

Last week Patti and I spent a night on the Castaway Caboose. It's part of a train ride in a remote area of West Virginia. They took us in our own private caboose for the night out along the tracks by the river, disconnected us, and left us alone for the night. As our campfire died and the last toasted marshmallow was consumed, God rolled out over us the wondrous heavenly carpet you see in the picture, and we began to *consider*.

I love to take the time to *consider*. Like the psalmist, I'm aware of the majesty of God and divine creation as well as my tiny, tiny place in that splendor. However, the psalmist makes a very important point. The wonder of it all is not meant to make me feel small and insignificant. The glory of God's creation is meant to remind me of the "glory and honor" with which I also have been made! As a child of God my life is just as important as the wonder and majesty of all the stars when I look to heaven.

When I stop to *consider* all of that I feel humbled and joyous. I can't help but respond to God with praise, thanksgiving, and a renewed commitment to fulfill my role as a servant of the one who cares so much. I pray that God will remind and invite me to stop my busyness from time to time to *consider*. How about you?

44

"... face to face ..."

"There on the mountain the Lord spoke to you face to face from the fire." (Deuteronomy 5:4)

I CHASED THESE GUYS all summer. Generally, I'd never see them until it was too late. As I walked along, they camouflaged themselves among the weeds then jumped further away as I approached. A few days ago I was delighted when this fellow jumped right in front of me on the sidewalk. (I think the falling temperatures made him a little sluggish.) I sprawled out on the sidewalk and there we were—face-to-face. I wonder what he wondered? I thought it was pretty special to lie there for a few moments and study him. (Patti managed to stand a few feet away and pretend she didn't know me.)

Anyway, face-to-face generally marks an important encounter. In the passage from Deuteronomy this face to face encounter between the Israelites and God provided the opportunity for the Ten Commandments to be communicated by God to Moses and the others. Businesses and governments recognize the importance of *face time*. Why else would executives and officials jet all around the world to meet each other face-to-face when a phone call or email would be so much simpler and cheaper?

Face-to-face time is important in relationships. Face-to-face is when we truly focus on one another. We see the subtle cues, the unvoiced hurts, joys, questions and more. We have the opportunity to respond in ways we otherwise might have missed were we not face-to-face. There is a connection face-to-face that is unique. The connection may be difficult to describe, but it is real and knowable. To seek out and meet one another face-to-face means that we really want to know the other. It communicates that we also really want to be known by the other. Face-to-face is the pathway to intimacy.

Too many relationships lack face-to-face time. There is no substitute. Many folks spend lots of time together, but still do not look for the opportunities to encounter each other face-to-face. It's really not enough to simply say, "I love you." If a relationship is to be intimate and fulfilling, I also have to want to know you. Truly knowing you comes from spending time with you face-to-face.

Our spiritual lives also require *face time* with God. It's not enough to say we believe. We also have to want to know and be known by God, and that also only comes from spending time face-to-face with God in worship, study, and prayer. I pray that God will remind me to seek the face-to-face time I need with God and others. How about you?

45

"... trust in you."

"When I am afraid, O Lord Almighty, I put my trust in you." (Psalm 56:3)

SOMETIMES TRUST IS EASY, sometimes it's difficult. A variety of situations have resulted in *trust* being the focus of the day for me. How fitting, then, that my day should end with a tremendous test of trust. Patti and I are in Chicago today and tomorrow so I can give a seminar on *teen depression* for the Illinois chapter of the National Association of Social Workers. We made a test run into the city this evening to scout out things and prepare for tomorrow. We walked around the block from the seminar venue and rode the express elevator to the top of the Willis Tower (formerly the Sears Tower).

At the observation level on the 103rd floor they have a rather unique experience. Extending about four feet from the side of the building are four glass boxes. The picture above shows my feet (and the rest of me) separated from the street about 1300 feet below by one and a half inches of glass. I am not a fan of heights! It took all the trust I could muster to inch my way out into the box and snap some photos! Sometimes trust is easy—and sometimes it is extremely difficult!

Trust is also precious. We are most aware of its value when we find it so difficult to trust. I envied the people with me on the observation platform that could just waltz out into the glass box, sit for a picture, and take joy in the sense of almost floating above the city. For me it was a teeth-gritting moment, but one I was determined to experience.

I'm not sure of the origin of my mistrust of heights. However, I know that many folks find it difficult to trust others because they have been betrayed and hurt one too many times. Sometimes just one betrayal can be enough to leave scars deep enough to make trusting others an experience just as teeth-gritting or worse than my few moments this evening.

". . . trust in you."

    Trust is precious. Trust can be lost. Trust can be regained. However, the wounds and scars can be horrific. We need to be so careful not to cause another to lose trust. The psalmist reminds us that God is the one to whom we should turn when we're afraid. It is God's consistent caring that makes this trust in divine help possible. That's what I celebrate and that's what I count on. I pray that God will help me be consistent in caring, and careful not to hurt in ways that might destroy an others trust. How about you?

46

"... merciful and tender ..."

"Our God is merciful and tender ..." (Luke 1:78)

PATTI AND I WERE on the road last week giving teen depression seminars. After driving 1700 miles and standing in a glass box on the side of the observation floor of the tallest building in the northern hemisphere it was

". . . merciful and tender . . ."

great to be home and have my feet firmly planted on the ground. While we were away a strong wind storm stripped most of the remaining leaves from these two giant oak trees that dwarf our home.

I enjoy the trees throughout the seasons as they display their many *looks*—spring green, summer shade, fall colors, winter snow laden, and this—just plain bare. I know for many this *just plain bare* look often conjures up images of strength as we are treated to a look at the magnificent trunk and branches that can support the weight of so many leaves. (I know the leaves are heavy because I dragged most of them to the waste pile before the windstorm). Just think of what the lumber from these trees could support. Oak radiates strength, whether standing as the stately trunk or supporting the roof of a barn.

For some reason I noticed something different this time as I surveyed this newly denuded pair. I focused on the delicate ends of the massive limbs. This same tree with such massive limbs that could probably support the weight of an elephant, can also nurture the tiniest of buds with tender shoots. Strength and tenderness are both part of the life cycle of a mighty oak tree.

Today, too many of the examples of *strength* are focused on almost brutish force. There's *strength* and then there's *tenderness*, we're told. Often we are led to believe that we must choose whether we're to be *strong* or whether we're to be *tender*. If we're strong there's little room for tenderness. In fact, tenderness is equated with weakness. If we're tender then how can we possibly show any strength? I'm convinced that true strength embraces tenderness.

That's exactly the model we see from God. The one whose strength calls life into being is the same one who shows mercy and tenderness in dealing with our hurt. The one who could destroy us is the one who offers grace by sending the Christ. Instead of being chased away and destroyed, we're invited into closer relationship.

Strength and tenderness are not an either/or. Strength embraces and embodies tenderness. Likewise, tenderness embraces and embodies strength. One without the other is even dangerous and destructive. I pray that God will show me the way of strength and tenderness. How about you?

47

"... depressed ..."

"Singing to a person who is depressed is like taking off a person's clothes on a cold day or like rubbing salt in a wound." (Proverbs 25:20)

ELVIS MOANED THROUGH A song about it—and many experience it—a *blue Christmas*. The blue lights around the flame in the photo reminded me of the song. In the midst of the time when lots of folks feel so wonderful and special there are those who feel so awful. Their experience can include grief from a loss, the *blues* for a few days, or clinical depression. Regardless of the form, it hurts—it really, really hurts. I think that's what the writer of Proverbs was trying to say in the verse below my photo, "Be careful with others because depression hurts." (Ironic, isn't it, a several hundred year old saying offering the same message as a current television commercial?) Depression hurts!

It's important that we recognize how much depression really hurts if we are to avoid rubbing salt in the wounds. Sometimes it's difficult for those of us who have never experienced clinical depression to understand just how much it hurts. The first step in turning from unhelpful to helpful ways of relating is trying to get a sense that the other person's depression really hurts. Depression is not something the person is making up or using to try and manipulate others. It is a dangerous illness that takes many lives each year. Clinical depression often needs professional help. Although the *blues* may not be as severe, the condition still requires patience and sensitivity on the part of those relating with the afflicted.

The Proverbs writer warns against forcing things upon the afflicted. Follow their lead. Allow the one with the blues to participate and be part of things without pushing them to feel like the rest of us. Try not to make them feel like they're a *party-pooper* if they're not in the holiday mood. Let them know you're aware of their feelings and want them around regardless of how they feel.

For those suffering through a *blue Christmas*, try to be careful not to listen to some of the distorted messages from the depression. You may have thoughts like, "I don't want to do anything," or, "I don't want to be around anyone." Those are not helpful thoughts.

Christmas is the season we celebrate God's healing light of hope coming into the world in the presence of Christ. God's healing love is made available in many ways—through the help of various professionals, through the joy of fellowship, and even through the off-key song of a tiny white robe-bedecked *angel* in a Christmas pageant. Make plans to participate with others, and let them carry God's healing light of hope for you to shine in the darkness of a *blue Christmas*. I pray that God will help me carry the healing light of hope for others and avoid rubbing salt in *blue wounds*. How about you?

48

"... a dim image in a mirror ..."

"*... a dim image in a mirror ...*"

"What we see now is like a dim image in a mirror; then we shall see face to face. What I know now is only partial; then it will be complete—as complete as God's knowledge of me." (I Corinthians 13:12)

Life is full of mystery. Would we want it any other way? As much as we need to know and want to know, wouldn't life be boring without some mystery? Science helps us discover the secrets of our world so we can better care for our lives and God's creation. Science helps us work with what is ... Faith invites us into what will be ... In relationships too much mystery can create a problem. If I don't know enough about you it might be difficult to trust. If I feel like you don't know me (or want to get to know me) then hurt might shatter our relationship.

Remember "The Newlywed Show" on television? Prizes were awarded to the newly married couple that knew the most trivial information about one another, like what brand of toothbrush the other used. What if we interviewed the winners five years into their marriages? Forget about toothbrushes. Would they know each other's deeper feelings? How many would fail the quiz?

We yearn to be known. It hurts enough to be at a place in life where we feel like we don't know anyone. It hurts even more to feel that we're not known by anyone. To feel *unknown* is deeply wounding, sometimes calling into question our very reason for living. "Who cares? Who would miss me?"

As we move toward Christmas remember that once more we're about to tell a story of mystery and wonder. At its core is a simple truth: God knows us fully, and cares enough to be with us. We are not alone. Thanks be to God! There are many *unknowns* among us who need to hear this good news. They may be next to us in our office, they may be next to us at the dinner table, or they may be living in a box under the bridge. I pray that God will help me seek and get to know those who feel *unknown*. How about you?

49

"... wait ..."

"But I will watch for the Lord; I will wait confidently for God, who will save me. My God will hear me." (Micah 7:7)

Advent involves a lot of waiting. That's exactly what this little fellow was up to—waiting among my Christmas lights for me to leave so it could swoop down and *snarf up* a few sunflower seeds in my feeder. We wait for the big day, we wait for the parties, we wait for the gifts, and we wait . . . for God?

For years I've taught and preached about waiting for God to surprise us, challenge us, and save us. Especially during Advent as we retell the story of God acting in Christ, we're reminded of the need to wait for God to speak to our need—our need for hope, our need for forgiveness, our need for peace. This Advent I find myself not just wondering about our waiting for God, but also, God's waiting for us. God is waiting for us to open ourselves to all the ways God's Spirit might be waiting to move with us and through us. Talk about exciting! But wait, there's more . . . I also think God is waiting for us to come to our senses.

Some things are almost impossible to do at the same time. It's impossible to smile and frown at the same time. It's impossible to hate and hold the Christ child at the same time. It's impossible to ignore those in need of help and hold the Christ child at the same time. We wait for the Christ child once more to bring God's Light into our darkness. God waits for us to come to our senses and realize we cannot embrace this Child and ignore our *neighbors* at the same time. We can only truly embrace this Child if we also embrace one another by seeking peace and justice for all!

As I wait for this Christmas I pray that God will challenge and prepare me to embrace the Christ child by repenting, then seeking peace and justice. How about you?

50

"... and little children will take care of them."

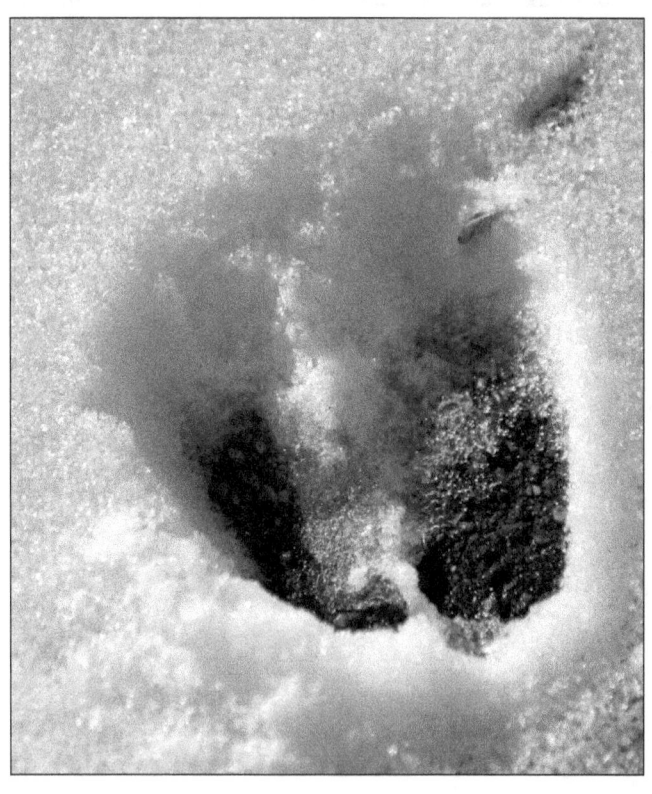

". . . and little children will take care of them."

"Wolves and sheep will live together in peace, and leopards will lie down with young goats. Calves and lion cubs will feed together, and little children will take care of them." (Isaiah 11:6)

THERE ARE REINDEER TRACKS all over my front lawn in the middle of my Christmas decorations! *Stop!* I don't want to hear your boring adult rationalizations reminding me these are just the tracks of the white-tail deer coming to graze on the carpet of acorns under our huge oak trees. It's December, it's almost Christmas, and we all should know what this means . . . *these are reindeer tracks!* That's exactly what my father pointed out to me when I was young and exactly what he and I pointed out to my children. So . . . *let's get excited for a change!!!*

Regardless of what some might say, Christmas is not merely for children. I wonder if people say and live that as an excuse to reduce the powerful message of God's radical kingdom of peace to a mere children's game? Christmas is not simply a chance to play like children with children and celebrate the joy of family. It's all that but so much more. Maybe if we reduce it to that sort of family party we wont' have to do the difficult, yet exciting loving that this Christ child wants to lead us to.

Christmas points us in the direction of the seemingly impossible becoming the possible. That's exactly what the prophet Isaiah meant when he said this Child would lead us into the Kingdom of God where the seemingly impossible—wolves hanging out with sheep, leopards schmoozing with goats, and lions consorting with cows would be a reality. In other words, God's love could bring peace where no one thought it possible.

Actually, we really do love being part of the impossible becoming possible. (Think reindeer flying, etc.) Why not accept the invitation of this Christ Child to be part of the excitement. Imagine loving the ones you thought or decided were unlovable . . . Wow! Let this Christmas be more than just a *family holiday*. Let this Christ Child lead us to God's exciting party—the Kingdom of Peace. I pray that God will help me accept this Christ Child's invitation. How about you?

51

"So watch what you do . . ."

"Jesus said to his disciples, 'Things that make people fall into sin are bound to happen, but how terrible for the one who makes them happen! It would be better for him if a large millstone were tied around his neck and he were thrown in to the sea then for him to cause one of these little ones to sin. So watch what you do!' . . ." (Luke 17:1–3)

"So watch what you do . . ."

I'VE WATCHED THIS FLOCK of geese long enough to tell you that the big guy in the middle is a real leader. If he decides to move to the other side of the lawn to forage for food, the other geese follow. If he gets a hankering to jump in the water and paddle downstream to a new site, the rest follow. The flock has learned the benefits of following in the footsteps of their leader, so they observe and copy his movements.

Learning to follow is a critical lesson for us to master very early in our lives. Many of our skills are developed when we are very young children by observing and copying—following. I even remember a cooking class in Cub Scouts where they emphasized *following*. They taught us how to cook simple things (hot dogs with cheese) then also gave us some tips on using good manners while dining. "When you're at a party and don't know which fork to use," they told us "just follow the lead of the hostess or host." How many times in the movies have you heard the line, "Just follow my lead?"

Following is important. We encourage it. When tragedy strikes like it has once more at the recent shootings in Tucson, AZ we must first realize that many factors are involved. In this situation it sounds like our lack of adequate mental health care is definitely one part of the complicated equation. However, it troubles me to hear that some think the spewing of hatred toward others has nothing to do with this kind of violence. We learn to follow. We encourage following. We teach each other to observe and copy—to follow. Then why are we so surprised in these tragedies that someone with other contributing factors like a form of mental illness that hinders their ability to make healthy decisions about whom and what to follow, winds up taking their cues from voices of hate that are readily offered as examples to copy?

It confounds me when I hear that folks think their angry tirades against one another or public figures have no impact on the behavior of others. We cannot hurl insult and injury toward one another and pretend it will not have an impact. We've been taught to follow—to observe and copy. The *leader* bears the responsibility for setting the example to be copied. That's exactly the warning Jesus was issuing to his disciples when he said, "So watch what you do!"

The *little ones* are watching—and looking to follow. We focus a lot of attention on proclaiming that individuals need to learn when and whom to follow. Some want to place all the responsibility on the followers. It's time we focused more attention on the examples we're offering for following.

Wednesday Wonderings

The examples we offer do make a difference. I pray that God will help me offer a healthy example. How about you?

52

"... endurance ..."

"Strive for righteousness, godliness, faith, love, endurance, and gentleness." (I Timothy 6:11)

I FOUND THESE PIGEONS all hunkered–down on the roof of a church not long ago, desperately trying to get through one of the coldest days of the winter. Seemed like there was little they could do except stay together, look for a warm roost on a roof where the building's heat might be escaping, and endure the season's blast of frigid air!

At first glance it seems almost strange to see the Apostle Paul list *endurance* with such other important traits as "godliness, faith, love and gentleness." Those strike me as much more active sorts of qualities, requiring healthy decision-making and self-control. Isn't *endurance* simply the only thing we can do when we can't really do anything? The other qualities sound as though they're born from strength while *endurance* reeks of leftovers and weakness. "All I can do is endure it," I've often heard spoken by someone in a time of pain and suffering!

So why did Paul include *endurance* in such a stellar list of qualities? Maybe it's because endurance is far more than the absence of anything that will fix our present condition. In fact, endurance is an act of faith in and of itself. Endurance requires we remember and celebrate in difficult times that God has gotten us through, and God will get us through. Endurance is not *all we have left*. Endurance is what we need.

There are more times in our lives than we would like to admit when we have little or no control of our circumstances. In those moments we are not powerless. Rather, we are emboldened to endure by the Spirit of God. I pray that God's Spirit will give me endurance. How about you?

53

"... hide ..."

"Those who try to hide their plans from the Lord are doomed! They carry out their schemes in secret and think no one will see them or know what they are doing." (Isaiah 29:15)

I WAS TAKING AN afternoon walk a couple of days ago when I looked up just in time to see the fellow in this picture perched on some cables stretched across the road from pole to pole. He had managed to wiggle his way through the wild grape vines that used the wires to traverse the road. I have to wonder if this guy thought he was truly hidden behind the vines because even when I walked right under him, he kept his perch without moving a muscle. We don't have *tame* squirrels in our neck of the woods, so most of them scramble away pretty quickly when approached. "Can't see me," he must have been saying to himself.

I remember sitting with a group of youth several years ago, listening to them discuss the proverbial question, "Is it okay to cheat?" I winced when I heard one say, "Sure, as long as you don't get caught." Sounds like a slightly older version of the child who stands alone in the kitchen, drooling over the plate of freshly baked chocolate chip cookies. Seeing and hearing no one, and convinced that his actions are hidden from mom and tattling siblings, he snitches a cookie and inhales it before running out of the room. I wonder how long it took him in his time-out chair to figure out that the slight smudge of chocolate on his cheek revealed the truth about the lie he had told his mother. "No, I didn't eat any cookies."

"Who sees us, who will know?" we ask ourselves as we prepare to hide our deeds in the darkness. Let's face it, if I had been a hunter with a shotgun instead of a camera, and if that squirrel had been trying to hide in those vines on a tree limb in the woods instead of a cable over the road by the church, he would have been stew meat in a matter of minutes. Our thinly veiled efforts to hide our deeds of the darkness are always much more vulnerable to failure than we want to believe. It's far easier for us to be *seen* than we imagine when our deeds of the darkness have us convinced that no one will see us and no will ever discover our indiscretions.

If we're not careful, our deeds of the darkness can convince us that no one will see us and no one will know, right up to the point (and even beyond) where we start to see our lives come crashing down around us. It's a very powerful and convincing voice in our heads that says, "Who sees us? Who will know?" One thing is for certain—it's not the voice of God. If we feel the urge or need to hide, we're probably not listening to the right voice. I pray that God will scream in my ear when the other voice tries to lead me to the darkness. How about you?

54

"... I did not reveal before."

"... Now I will tell you of new things to come, events that I did not reveal before." (Isaiah 48:6)

Wednesday Wonderings

FOR ALMOST THIRTY YEARS this milky white stained-glass bird with just a slight sheen of color on one surface has hung in the window of every one of my offices. It was fashioned as a gift by a talented parishioner and has traveled with me from West Virginia, to Massachusetts, then on to Virginia—and finally, back to West Virginia. In my present office it hangs a little differently. Instead of dangling right up against the windowpane as it did in the other offices, it swings from fishing line a few inches in front of the window. That's what helped set up the discovery in the photo. Last week I walked into the office just at the right moment to see for the very first time the *rainbow bird* projected on the wall jutting out from the window. Wow! What a discovery after almost thirty years of watching the bird in the window!

Frankly, I've never been that fond of the bird. Of the several beautiful things the same parishioner made for me, this bird has never been my favorite. I've always treasured it, but more for its meaning and less for its beauty. It just seemed so plain old plain . . . until last week.

We all form opinions about one another, and our actions and interactions generally follow from those opinions. I'm convinced that most of our opinions of each other are based more on what we don't know rather than what we really know of one other. This week I'm meeting as part of a board to interview candidates for ministry. As we progress through the interviews I'm reminded of what hard work it is to discover the unknowns of our candidates and make our best efforts to get to know them before making decisions.

It is hard work to get to know one another and to keep on discovering the hidden treasures and new revelations throughout the life of the relationship. Maybe we do some of our worst hurting of each other when we first stop the hard work of discovery and become content to live in the stagnant pools of assumption. Through Isaiah God offered hope with new revelations, new manifestations of God's capacity to love even when disappointed by us. The more we work to know God, the more we know of divine love and hope. The more we work to know each other, the less likely we are to inflict wounds and more likely we are to share divinely inspired Christ-like love. I pray that God will give me the energy and discipline to continue the hard work of discovery and avoid the pitfalls of assumption. How about you?

55

"... release ..."

"The Sovereign Lord has filled me with his Spirit. He has chosen me

Wednesday Wonderings

and sent me to bring good news to the poor, to heal the broken-hearted, to announce release to captives and freedom to those in prison." (Isaiah 61:1)

It's probably safe to say that most folks in our country today are ready to cry out to *Old Man Winter* in one united voice of frustration, "Release us!" Whew, it's been a rough winter in most parts of the country. I thought about that a few days ago as I watched the icicles on our house begin to thaw and break away. In the split second captured by my camera in the photo above we're witnessing the miraculous *release* of water that had been bound up as ice. The drops oozing from their frozen, suspended state of animation can splat upon the ground, be absorbed into the soil, and once more join in the greater movements of water that help sustain life for God's spectacular creation. Wow!

I continue to be amazed at how easy it is for us to be frozen and imprisoned by our anger, fear, greed, ignorance, anxiety, stubbornness, prejudice, misunderstanding, addiction, denial, pain, suffering, depression, or more. (Whew, that's quite a list). Obviously, there are many, many different ways we can find ourselves stuck, unable to move from our state of frozen suspension. Sometimes we know we're *stuck*, but we remain stuck in our prison because *we* can't see the answer. *We* can't see how we could move from our present condition to a healthier state, so we remain stuck. We may know that the state we're in is not healthy, and possibly hurtful to others, but since *we* haven't been able to figure out how to free ourselves, we remain in our *frozen* state. We figure if *we* can't see the way out, then there must not be a way out.

"When all else fails, read the directions," goes a popular saying of our time. In other words, turn for help. Maybe that's exactly what Isaiah meant when he said that God would bring release to the captives. Instead of remaining stuck, instead of concluding and settling with the idea that living in a state of frozen *stuckness* is the only answer—*ask for help*. I pray that when my feet are frozen in some state of fear, anger, hurt, or whatever, God will remind me to ask for divine help so I might be released by Christ's love and return to the nourishing flow of God's gift of life. How about you?

56

"The water is up to my neck..."

"Save me, O God! The water is up to my neck..." (Psalm 69:1)

ONCE MORE THE HEAVY rains have flooded the bottom near the creek, threatening to choke the life from the trees that call it home. Rising, muddy waters raise anxiety and fear about damage and destruction. If you've ever lived in a flood-prone area you know that with each encroachment of the waters there come the same sort of questions, "How far will it get this time? Do you think it will reach us this time? Can we endure another flood and the awful mess and heartache the receding waters will leave behind? Will we make it this time?"

It seems there are those who endure frequent *flooding* in their lives from things other than rising storm waters and ask the same questions. "Save me, O God! The water is up to my neck," cries the psalmist when crisis threatens once again. It's difficult when we encounter another who seems prone to flooding, whose life seems overwhelmed by crisis after crisis. As many times as I've faced those situations with others and waded with them through many a flood, I find it's still difficult to resist those first impulses to judge, to avoid, and run. It never gets any easier to wade into muddy waters, even though I consider it a sacred privilege to have the opportunity, and am always blessed in the journey.

A favorite philosophical question of our age goes something like, "If a tree falls in a forest (or flood waters) and no one is around to hear it, does it make a sound?" What folks have taught me through their suffering is that the most dangerous time is when the flood waters rise and they feel like no one is with them, that their cries are no longer heard, that they might as well not even exist. That's when it's easiest to fall into the murkiness of the depths and be swept away forever. The psalmist cries out because he knows God hears the cry.

I've waded through floods with others and been told they've cried out but haven't felt like God was listening. I've known those moments as well, but have survived a few floods to find later that God was listening, even when I thought otherwise. It seems to help that person when I can offer the assurance of my experience and the assurance of my presence. What I've also found is that God has used my efforts and testimony to offer the assurance of divine presence in those moments. I pray that God will give me the will to wade into the waters where someone is crying. How about you?

57

"Go to the Lord for help . . ."

"Go to the Lord for help; and worship him continually." (Psalms 105:4)

IT WAS ALMOST EXACTLY five years ago that Patti and I finished our nine months *on the road* and began our trek back to the east coast to begin our new jobs. She had just finished working nine months as a travel nurse at a

Wednesday Wonderings

couple of different hospitals while I took a sabbatical to write a book on *teen depression*. We began our journey home from Oregon by way of the state of Washington. I took the picture above from the Visitor's Center at Mount St. Helens. The black and white smoke contains the ashes and steam that continue to arise from this active volcano. In 1980 the 12,000 ft. volcano erupted, blowing off about 4,000 ft., roughly a chunk of debris about the size of Spruce Knob, the highest mountain in West Virginia. Below is the 8,000 ft. that's left of Mt. St. Helens.

The picture of the smoldering crater hangs on my office wall along with several others. Sometimes folks comment on the photos, and I tell them it's my *Spirit Wall*. The photos depict the moments I have stood in various places and felt the presence of God's Holy Spirit saying, "I Am." I look at the photos from time to time and, "Go to the Lord for help . . ." Then I feel God's presence!

Yesterday I was wandering through a large store killing time while Patti was *shopping*. I realized the music coming over the store's system was basically an *elevator music version* of popular contemporary Christian music and older hymns. Just about the same time I rounded the corner and saw about a fourteen-inch print of a cross, covered in pink leopard-skin print. "Yuck," I thought to myself. "This whole music and cross thing is awful."

Then I heard the Spirit say again, "I Am," in a slightly different way. I heard God confronting me about my *ism*. You know what I mean, it wasn't rac*ism*, or sex*ism*, but it was certainly some sort of *ism*. I *can* feel God on a mountaintop or some other awesome place. I *wasn't* feeling that same sort of presence with elevator music and a pink leopard-skin-print cross—but

"Go to the Lord for help . . ."

someone else might have been . . . I think our *isms* must live right on the tip of our tongues because it sure doesn't take much to hear our selves voice them. I need to experience the strength of the Lord that comes from knowing divine presence. I don't expect I'll ever experience it through a pink leopard-skin-print cross—but who knows?

Seek the Lord's presence, but don't ever limit the possibilities for how God will choose to reveal divine love. After all, how outrageous is it to find love on a cross in the first place? I pray that God will continue to give me his strength through his presence—in whatever form that might take (but I'd still rather it be a majestic mountain instead of elevator music and pink leopard-skin print.) I also pray that God will help me control my *isms* before they have the chance to hurt another. How about you?

58

"... sets you free ..."

"*... sets you free ...*"

"If the Son sets you free, then you will be really free." (John 8:36)

SOME CALL IT "SHROVE Tuesday," others "Pancake Day," and others "the last day of Mardi Gras." As for me, it's "Toasty Tuesday." That's because each year on the day before Ash Wednesday I get my blackened metal bucket and wad up inside it all the leftover dried palm branches from the previous Palm Sunday celebration. Then I thoroughly douse it with some charcoal lighter fluid, then add a little more, and then add a little more, and then add a little more ... (You get the picture). I stand back a respectful distance, light the match, toss it into the bucket ... and *whoosh* ... I love to watch the flames soar into the air, like hands reaching out to heaven. In only a matter of moments the palm limbs that once graced a tree and added to its beauty, limbs that might have provided shade to a passer-by, limbs that eventually helped tell the story of Jesus' triumphant entry into Jerusalem, are now nothing more than ashes at the bottom of my sooty bucket.

Each year my *Toasty Tuesday* celebration helps remind me of the precious nature of this gift of life, and also reminds me of the need for endings and freedom—the need for moving on. As the branches burn I'm reminded that another year has passed since my last celebration. In that year many things have come to pass, some joyful, some sorrowful, some edifying, and some hurtful. When we hurt we need to know there is hope for release and freedom. When we rejoice with success we need to know there is hope for future success. There comes a time to *move on* if we are to avoid getting stuck in either the pain of the hurtful, or the potential stagnation of the joyful. For me my *Toasty Tuesday* celebrations remind me of just that.

For those of us who are Christians, Lent provides us the preparation time necessary to move on. The ashes we use today, Ash Wednesday, remind us that for all our joys and all our failures we are children of the loving God who provides the way to move on through the love shown in Jesus Christ. I pray that God's Spirit will confront me with the need and show me the way to keep moving on so I can be part of the world's transformation by God's grace. How about you?

59

"... wings like eagles..."

"... wings like eagles..."

"Even those who are young grow weak; young people can fall exhausted. But those who trust in the Lord for help will find their strength renewed. They will rise on wings like eagles; they will run and not get weary; they will walk and not grow weak." (Isaiah 40:30-31)

Patti and I were just beginning our trip back home from Richmond, VA on Saturday morning. I had given a teen depression seminar the day before. We were both tired and not really looking forward to the long drive ahead, when suddenly, Patti gave out a cry, "I think I just saw a hawk, no, an eagle by the road!" Since it wasn't an interstate highway I was able to quickly turn the car around, and sure enough, there was this beautiful creature. Our whole day was blessed by just that one moment when Patti spotted the eagle.

Life can take such a dramatic change in the fleetest of moments. A rumbling earthquake, a rushing tsunami, or even the gravest of bad news can turn life upside down, inside out, leaving a wide swath of despair in its path. It only takes a moment... Yet life is so much more than any single moment. Maybe that's the message of eagles' wings. They are strong and powerful, capable of carrying this creature of God through the stormy blast and into the miracle of many other God-given moments.

It only takes a moment for bad news or destruction to convince us that life can never be good or meaningful ever again. In the aftermath of those moments it is vital that we remember God's promise of eagles' wings. Friday, I needed a sign, and this eagle was certainly God's sign for me! I pray that especially in *those* moments God will remind me and help me remind others of eagles' wings. How about you?

60

"... walked in darkness ..."

"The people who walked in darkness have seen a great light..." (Isaiah 9:2 and Matthew 4:16)

PATTI AND I WERE hiking through the canyons of Zion National Park in Utah when this scene opened before us. The shadowed trail we were travers-

". . . walked in darkness . . ."

ing was just a turn in the path away from the glorious sun drenched canyon walls before us. So close . . . The Light is oh so close . . . but sometimes seems so far away. In our Christian calendar we proclaimed the coming of the Light at Christmas and now find ourselves wandering through Lent.

It struck me that this photo is a good representation of Lent. We see the Light from the darkness of our lives, but now we have to choose to take those last few steps and cross over into the Light in order for its healing and comfort to engulf us. Lent is about choice. We must make the conscious effort to step into the Light. Fear, anger, cynicism, and even misguided pleasure can keep us on the fringe looking at the Light but not walking in the Light. Lent is about choice—and Hope.

The sweetest candy is tasteless and worthless as long as it lies on the shelf wrapped tightly in cellophane. (Trust me, I have a raging sweet tooth and know these things!) Walking *near* the Light is similar. It *looks* great, but . . . Take the step . . . walk *in*, not *near* the Light. I pray that God will give me the courage to choose to take the step *into* the light of divine healing and hope. How about you?

61

"... a fierce storm ..."

"Suddenly a fierce storm hit the lake, and the boat was in danger of sinking. But Jesus was asleep." (Matthew 8:24)

LAST WEDNESDAY I STOPPED long enough to snap this photo right before I went into our local television station to do an interview on the 5:00PM news. About ten minutes later I watched out a window as one of the hardest hailstorms I have ever witnessed rushed through the area. I fully expected to go out after the interview and find my car cratered like the moon. (Thankfully there was no damage.)

I've been through several storms in my life both personally and professionally. Looking back I realize I've been pummeled at various times by some pretty hard emotional and spiritual pellets. Early in my career as a minister, during one particular storm that overwhelmed me about as quickly as this front in the photo moving through last Wednesday, I remember leaning against a tree in the woods all by myself (except for the cold, lifeless body of one of my youth group members lying a few feet away) and praying (screaming) to God, "I quit."

I'm certain there was quite a lot of screaming when the disciples found Jesus asleep in the boat during a raging, life-threatening storm. Surviving in a storm can be messy and intense. Our prayer life may even reflect the messiness and intensity of our situation with outcries of pain and suffering. Don't worry! God can handle our intensity and messiness!

When the disciples cried out to the sleeping Jesus in the midst of the storm, he heard them and spoke to their need. When I shouted out to God, "I quit," in the midst of my storm, God heard me and spoke to my need. I heard God's voice offer me peace, hope, patience, and challenge. I'm still a minister and pastoral counselor some 30 years after that particular *storm* so obviously God got me through that storm and several others!

Philosophers, theologians, and the rest of us have debated for centuries and centuries about why *storms* (*bad things*) happen. For now I have decided that my simple answer to that question is, "I don't know. Someday I plan to ask God face to face." Until then here's what I can tell you about storms. First, God hears us in the midst of them. Knowing that I'm *heard* means more than I can describe in this simple offering. Suffice it to say that being heard gives me the encouragement I need to get through the storm. That brings me to the second thing I *do* know about storms. God gets us through. That's what I've found, and that's what I'm sharing! I pray that God will help me share the Good News: God hears us in the storms and God gets us through the storms! How about you?

62

"... ashamed ..."

"I write this to you, not because I want to make you feel ashamed, but to instruct you as my own dear children."(I Corinthians 4:14)

Something told me not to get too attached when I discovered this mother goose on her nest a couple of weeks ago. She and her mate had constructed a nice nest on its own little island in the middle of the creek. The mother patiently perched upon the nest while the expectant father hovered a few feet away. Every once in awhile she stood up to reveal the eggs she was safekeeping. Then came the rains. . . and more rains. . . and more rains.

Today I returned to find the nest abandoned with the waters of the creek flowing almost at the base of the pile of brush the geese had formed to hold their brood. There were no geese to be seen. Frankly, I think the nest was flooded. It looks like the geese picked the wrong spot at the wrong time. They made a mistake, a terrible mistake that apparently cost them dearly.

When the Apostle Paul wrote to the people of Corinth who were members of the early Christian church he had a lot on his mind to share with them. Apparently there had been some pretty big mistakes that had been made and needed correcting. It's interesting (and important) that Paul included in his admonishments and teaching, "I write this to you, not because I want to make you feel ashamed, but to instruct you as my own dear children." Paul knew the power of shame, its ability to trap and destroy instead of instruct and heal.

We all make mistakes, even big mistakes that can cost us dearly. If our response to a mistake is to feel ashamed, the shame makes us feel like we *are* a mistake instead of feeling that we've *made* a mistake. That's why Paul impressed upon the Corinthians that his goal was to instruct them, not shame them. Shame causes us to want to duck and run to avoid the terrible feeling of *being* a mistake. Then we're left alone in our shameful prison. Instruction invites us to consider the mistake we *made* so we might learn from it, be forgiven for it, and be free to grow in relationships through it.

Lent is about instruction, not shame. God invites us to consider our mistakes, our bent to sinning, not so we can be shackled by shame, but rather, so we might be lovingly instructed by grace and invited once more into relationship with God through Christ. God knows the power of shame and offers grace in Christ to combat it. It is extremely easy for us to shame rather than instruct one another. I pray that I can accept God's grace to combat my own shame, and carefully instruct rather than shame others. How about you?

63

"... a witness ..."

"For you will be a witness for him to tell everyone what you have seen and heard." (Acts 22:15)

"... *a witness* ..."

WE WERE DRIVING THROUGH Davis, West Virginia last Saturday when suddenly Patti said, "Look at that tree in the chimney!" "What?" I replied as I pulled the car over to snap the pictures I knew I had to have in my collection. It was true, bigger than life, or was it? Something nagged at me as I thought about sharing the picture. "Is this real, or a really good hoax, something like an internet gag waiting for me to fall victim and then feel pretty stupid when my naiveté was revealed. So . . . I hesitated to show the photos.

Then it hit me, "The post office is in that building. Why not call someone in that office and ask them about the tree?" A very friendly gentleman on the other end of the phone was quick to explain that the tree was no hoax. He shared his concern that the tree had been growing there for a couple of years and if something was not done about it pretty soon the roots probably would take down the chimney. His theory was that a bird or the wind probably had deposited the seed that had grown into the chimney-splitting tree perched three stories above the ground. Pretty amazing if you ask me!

Now I'm really delighted to share the photos, but before speaking to the postal clerk I was ready to keep them to myself. I needed a witness to their authenticity before I was willing to believe and share. The Apostle Paul was recruited to be a witness to the miracle of God's love that was being revealed in this Jesus. God is busy at work all around us, but some of the most amazing examples of that love go *unnoticed* because they seem too much of a stretch. "Can God really love me that much . . . no . . . couldn't be . . ." Sometimes it just feels like too much of a stretch . . . maybe just a long perpetuated hoax . . .

Sometimes we need a witness, someone who can tell us this *too good to be true* forgiving and reconciling God is for real. Sometimes we need a witness to tell us that what we want to believe but are afraid to believe for fear of further disappointment is, in fact, true. God really is ready and able to love us back into wholeness and new life!

Apparently trees can grow out of chimneys. I have that from a reliable witness. God can love us back into life from death. Sometimes we all need a witness to believe and claim that love. I thank God for the witnesses that have shared their experiences of this amazing love for me, and pray that I, too, can be a witness to that divine love I have seen and heard. How about you?

64

"... liars and deceivers..."

"Save me, Lord, from liars and deceivers." (Psalm 120:2)

THIS PAST WEEK PATTI and were in Houston, Texas so I could give some talks on teen depression and other topics. One afternoon we were able to get away and engage in one of our favorite activities, a walk on the beach, this one at Galveston. We've walked many beaches on the east, west, and gulf coasts, but never before had we encountered the sight before us—piles and piles of brown seaweed filled with these iridescent *balloons*.

Wednesday Wonderings

Something told me to be careful around these beautiful creatures. At first I thought they were jellyfish, but then I realized they weren't really *jelly*. In fact, they looked just like latex balloons (and sounded like them when Patti popped one with a stick). I pushed a couple of them over and saw some interesting tentacles hanging from the bottom. Hmm . . . pretty on top, but something sinister on the bottom . . .

"Don't let looks deceive you," certainly applied in this case. These were Portuguese Men-of-War, beautiful, almost inviting to play with, but deceitfully hiding tentacles full of venom capable of killing small animals. The venom is even dangerous after the *balloons* have settled on the beach and died. Whew, good thing we only poked them with sticks!

The psalmist warns of liars and deceivers. It's easy to tell a lie. Sometimes a lie just gets blurted out in an impulsive moment of anxiety, anger, etc. Deceit seems even worse because it requires some planning. A *web of deceit* is constructed often times to hide or misrepresent the truth. Deceit inevitably hurts in order to gain its goal.

We've all been the victims of deceitful ploys by others. Somewhere along the line we probably fell into some *trap* because we believed too much and tested too little. We walked away feeling *stung*, rubbing our wounds, and vowing, "We won't be fooled again!"

The worst webs of deceit I have ever seen are the ones we spin for ourselves. Recently I was talking with someone recovering from an addiction.

They said, "You just don't see it (the truth of how you're hurting yourself and others) while you're in it." They're right. The web of deceit we spin for ourselves can hide our own troubling behaviors and attitudes, leaving us to blame others for our troubles. From within that web of deceit it appears obvious to us that our difficulties are the fault of someone else, so obviously, how can we be expected to change anything?

Easter is an invitation to accept a new life—a life lived in truth and love. God knows the truth about us and loves us anyway. That's what Jesus' life, death, and resurrection truly mean. Beware of lies and deceit, and accept the invitation to new life. I pray that God will give me the courage to seek the truth and willingness to accept the invitation to new life. How about you?

65

"... will not overwhelm you ..."

"When you pass through deep waters, I will be with you; your troubles will not overwhelm you ..." (Isaiah 43:2)

My week began with one of those family medical emergencies eliciting a "Whuuuuuuuuu," sort of response. You know what I mean. You hear the sharp inward sucking of air passing through your lips and throat as your brain starts to play ninety million different scenarios about the possible future consequences of the emergency.

Then today, just as I got off the phone from hearing some good news about the situation I heard the sweet voice of my loving wife calling up from the basement (rather calmly, all things considered), "Dear, the basement is flooded. The sump pump quit working." Once again I heard the, "Whuuuuuuuuu," as I surveyed the extent of the water's meanderings.

In both circumstances I thought of the photo above that I took a few years ago while we were visiting one of the Great Lakes. Why, because in both situations this week I had to do the same thing as when I stood at the bottom of those stairs. I had to remind myself several times to just take one small step at a time. Even though I knew I would have to go back up the steps in the photo as I descended them to get a great shot of the lighthouse on the cliff, the stairs were still daunting as I began to ascend. "Just take it one step at a time," I told myself.

Many times in my life I've found myself at the bottom of one of one of those flights of stairs, starting to feel overwhelmed as I contemplated the future. It's a tenuous position, because unless we're able to shift that seemingly overwhelming flight of stairs into a simpler *one step at a time* scenario, we might not take even the first step. Maybe it seems too simple—but it works!

Wednesday Wonderings

It works for me because I feel the voice of God reminding me, "When you pass through deep waters I will be with you . . ." That too, may seem too simple, but it's true. God's sustaining presence at the bottom of the stairs and through each step is what gives me the ability to coach myself with, "Just take it one step at a time." Ultimately, my anxiety is lowered, my anger is calmed, my frustration is abated, and my peace is restored. I can get through—I can climb the stairs—I will not be overwhelmed. I pray that God will help me take the next step. How about you?

66

"... lose my strength..."

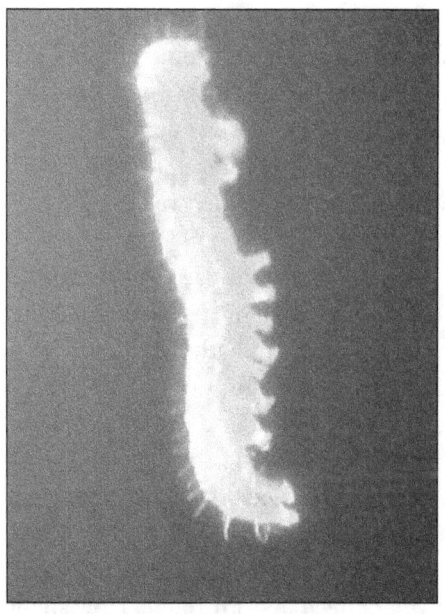

"She (Delilah) kept on asking him, day after day. He (Samson) got so sick and tired of her bothering him about it that he finally told her the truth. 'My hair has never been cut,' he said. 'I have been dedicated to God as a nazirite from the time I was born. If my hair were cut, I would

Wednesday Wonderings

lose my strength and be as weak as anybody else.'" (Judges 16:17)

Yesterday I was outside moving boxes around from our flooded basement and was surprised by this tiny one-inch-long critter appearing suddenly in my path. He was quickly making his way up his *rope* from the ground to a tree branch about ten feet above. Wow, what strength! If my math is correct, that works out proportionally to me hoisting my body straight up a rope about 700 feet, a seventy-story building. (Fat chance of that ever happening!) That's some strong caterpillar!

Ever lose your strength or have the wind knocked out of your sails? We know it happened to Samson. He gave in, told Delilah his secret, she cut his hair, and he lost his strength. I remember as a young boy going to see this story portrayed in a Hollywood movie. A lot of it went right over my very young head (like all the romantic stuff between Samson and Delilah), but the end made a dramatic impact. Samson returned to God, and his strength was restored.

There are lots of ways to lose our strength or the *wind in our sails*. Sometimes it's of our own doing, and sometimes it's just the end result of circumstances over which we have little or no control. The resulting situation is the same. We feel *becalmed*, just like a ship bobbing in the middle of the ocean without the power to move in the direction we need or want to travel. "How will I ever get through?" we may ask ourselves. "How will I ever find the strength again?"

When I find myself *becalmed* I often remember difficult times from the past that I've later wondered how in the world I got through. I realize that in those situations I found strength that I know was not my own, otherwise I would have lost the strength to continue and remained *becalmed*. The strength I found came from God, no doubt about it. It's important when we find ourselves *becalmed* to actively turn our thoughts toward the Lord and seek the strength we need that we cannot create for ourselves. If we don't make an active effort, we risk remaining becalmed and falling into despair. When I lose my strength I pray that I will remember to return to the Lord and find what I need to get through. How about you?

67

"You never know . . ."

"You never know when your time is coming. Like birds suddenly caught in a trap, like fish caught in a net, we are trapped at some evil moment when we least expect it." (Isaiah 9:12)

Wednesday Wonderings

JUST TWO DAYS AGO I watched folks picnicking in the riverfront park and launching their fishing boats for a day of angling. Today, it's raining *again* and suddenly the Ohio River is flooding its banks *again*. As the promotional posters for the series of *Jaws* movies once proclaimed, "Just when you thought it was safe to go back in the water..."

How vulnerable we truly are as human beings! We expect a certain amount of strain and stress in life, but disasters that suddenly surprise us without warning can be especially devastating. Our first response is most often shock, almost like a state of suspended animation in which we might feel frozen or numb and find it difficult to get our brain wrapped around the reality of what has just happened to us. When we exit the shock we might discover ourselves overwhelmed by the rush of many different, intense feelings, almost like the *feeling* returning to a limb after it's *fallen asleep* from our keeping it in an awkward position. Physically, emotionally, and spiritually our successful recovery from disaster is based not just on what we do after the fact, but also on the preparations we made before the calamity.

I remember as a child living in a perennially flood-prone area. It was before the days of bottled water. If the river was rising residents were warned to fill all their containers and bathtubs with water before the area's treated water supply became tainted and disrupted by rising waters and flooded pumping stations. Having water after the flood to quench our thirst could depend on how well we prepared by filling our reservoirs before the disaster.

Our own survival as well as our ability to help others through and after disasters also can depend on how well we heeded the call to fill our emotional and spiritual reservoirs before the crisis. Have we cultivated and nourished good relationships with family, friends, co-workers, and neighbors? Have we nurtured a relationship with our God whose story in the scriptures testifies to divine love that gets us through time and time again? We may not be able to foretell or forestall some disasters. However, the choices we make in our day to day living with one another and God may prove a major difference in how we emerge from the next disaster. I pray that God will help me keep the *reservoirs* filled. How about you?

68

"... leaving..."

"At daybreak Jesus left the town and went off to a lonely place. The people started looking for him, and when they found him, they tried to keep him from leaving. But he said to them, 'I must preach the Good News about the Kingdom of God in other towns also, because that is what God sent me to do.'" (Luke 4:42-43)

Wednesday Wonderings

A YOUTH FROM OUR church showed me the nest in a bush by the corner of the building. Mama robin had tucked the nest just inside the branches, but pretty much at eye level, making for some very amazing bird watching. By the time I took this picture the three little birds were not quite so little and looked pretty uncomfortable all squished together. Let's face it leaving the nest is difficult.

As a matter of fact, most transitions are difficult, be they a graduation, new birth, divorce, death, move to a new location, or promotion. Even the ones that include joy, anticipation, and excitement can also include more difficult feelings like anxiety, fear of the unknown, and sadness. Whoever said, "A bird in the hand is worth two (or three) in the bush," knew what they were saying. It can be very difficult to leave that nest of familiarity and fly into the future of possibilities.

When we're faced with transitions we often focus on the negatives or dangers of leaving and stepping into the unknown. What about the negatives and dangers of staying? Take another look at those three little guys in the photo. If they stay much longer they'll literally suffocate one another.

In the Gospel of Luke we hear a story of how villagers were so taken by Jesus and his work among them that they tried to keep him from leaving. Jesus could have stayed in the comfort of the villagers' adoration. Instead, he left because he knew that staying would mean the danger of his purpose on earth not being fulfilled. "I must preach the Good News about the Kingdom of God in other towns also, because that is what God sent me to do," Jesus said. The temptation to stay was great, but the need to go was greater.

We know from the rest of the Gospels that Jesus faced many transitions in the ensuing months. We also know that he was able to stay *on the move* because he felt the presence of God with him. That's the promise for us as well.

Leaving or moving on is difficult. The comfort of the nest and/or the awkward, painful, ominous feelings of change can sometimes convince us to stay when we should be leaving or moving on. Listen for God's Spirit working within you, giving courage for first, faltering new steps and strength for the journey. I pray that God will help me have the patience and grace to stay and courage to move when called in either direction. How about you?

69

"... hated their brother ..."

"When his brothers saw that their father loved Joseph more than he loved them, they hated their brother so much that they would not speak to him in a friendly manner."(Genesis 37:4)

Wednesday Wonderings

WHEN I SAW THESE two spider webs *posted* side-by-side on the fence yesterday morning I couldn't help but wonder if there was some sort of friendly competition or sibling rivalry going on. It's happened to me on more than one occasion that a child has asked me to judge their artwork as being the *best of show*, even while I'm surrounded by other children holding their own creations. The best I can usually muster is something like, "Oh, it's wonderful. I think all the drawings are wonderful," and pray the child doesn't press me any further to declare a *winner*.

We all have it as young children, that deep need to be *special* or *the best*. Millions, if not billions, are spent each year on ribbons, trophies, and the like to support that need to feel like *we're number one*. Every child in the very early stages of their development needs to see themselves reflected in the admiring gaze of those who lovingly hold them and feel that they are, indeed, most special. Sometimes with our children I think we confuse the need to feel special with a need to compete. All the trophies in the world can never compare with the signs and words of affirmation we as adults can offer our children on a daily basis. A little competition is fine, but it was never meant to fulfill that need to feel special, the kind of feeling we crave and can only be truly fulfilled when we're in relationship with others who make us feel loved. (Honestly, sometimes I think parents should focus more on playing with their children and a little less on getting them involved in every sort of competitive opportunity that comes along.)

As adults we also carry with us that need to feel special. We yearn to feel special somehow to someone. That's what lights us up in romantic relationships. I think it also lies behind some of our drive to compete as adults, even if we compete simply by backing a certain sports team. If our team wins we feel special. "We're number 1," we scream, even if *we* never stepped foot on the field. It's important that we acknowledge this need to feel special. If not, we risk the emptiness we feel without it driving us into bitter feelings and hurtful behaviors.

In the passage from Genesis above, we see how the brothers of Joseph reacted when they were not made to feel special by their father. They hated Joseph and followed those destructive feelings to an act of murderous proportions. On a more contemporary note, I remember in the comedy routine of the Smothers Brothers when Tom would be losing an argument with his more articulate brother, Dick, and finally would play his trump card by saying, "Mom always liked you best!" It was a funny line, but probably struck a chord with adults not because we all had mothers that favored

> "... hated their brother..."

one of our siblings, but because we could identify with that need to feel special—even as adults.

We do not need to ignore or deny this need to feel special. In fact, I think it's when we try to ignore or deny it that we wind up looking for it to be fulfilled in unhealthy relationships and behaviors. God knows our need and responds by loving each of us as though we are the only ones God has to love. That's one way to think about God sending the Holy Spirit to be with us after Jesus—that God came to love all of us in Jesus, and dwell most specially with each of us in the Holy Spirit. Our response to God's gift is to love as we have been loved, to affirm each other as special children of God. I pray that God will help me love, just as I am loved. How about you?

70

"... presence..."

"I am always aware of the Lord's presence; he is near, and nothing can shake me." (Psalm 16:8)

I REALIZE THIS MAY sound crazy, but I watched these two tree swallows (at least I think they're tree swallows) at their nest for a few moments at a

"... *presence* ..."

nearby pond and was immediately transported back in time to the day I spent in the labor and delivery room with my wife as she struggled through many hours of labor to give birth to our son. In spite of all the classes we attended where I was affirmed as such an important part of the birthing process, when push came to shove (no pun intended because the birth wound up being a caesarean section) I still felt like my wife was doing all the work and I was simply hanging out. Makes me wonder if the mama bird in my photo was looking out to make sure her *hubby* was still there, half expecting that he had gotten bored with all the waiting and flown off for some distractions. Why was she checking? Was his presence actually important even though there wasn't much for him to do but wait?

There is no substitute for the presence of another sharing the pain and joy of life. Media, electronics, and other distractions may occupy our attention for awhile but none can ever take the place of the assurance and peace that comes from the awareness of that other sitting or standing next to you in good times and others. Yet, sometimes I still have to check myself when that *practical* bone in my brain vibrates and says, "Well, there's nothing you can do, so . . ." Our helplessness and awkwardness can be so powerful that they can make us want to fly away when all that is needed from us is our presence.

We take for granted the gift of God's presence with us when we fail to share our presence with one another. I've been known to remind my congregation during a worship service that their presence is important to someone sitting among us that day. We might not know what difficulty the person is facing, but that person walked through the door that morning hoping to experience the presence of God and the presence of the gathered. *Unshakable* is how the psalmist says it feels to be aware of the Lord's presence.

What a gift God has given us, and what a gift we have to share with one another—the presence of God in our shared presence with one another! I pray that God will help me appreciate the gift I've been given by sharing the gift of *presence* with others. How about you?

71

"... watching..."

"The Lord is always watching what people do; everything they do is as clear as day to him... But the Lord will allow those who repent to return to him. He always gives encouragement to those who are losing hope." (Sirach 17:19 and 24) (One of the Apocryphal books of the Old Testament)

". . . watching . . ."

I WAS SLOWLY CIRCLING the green-slime-covered pond watching for signs of life to photograph when I saw from a distance this *log* sticking up out of the water. Drawing closer to that part of the pond I watched the *log* submerge beneath the surface. That's when I realized I wasn't the only one doing the watching. I was being watched by one of the huge snapping turtles that claimed this emerald pond as their home. A few moments later I stood still, he resurfaced, and we spent several moments quietly watching each other.

The author of Sirach says that the Lord is always watching us, waiting to see whether we'll take a path toward health and wholeness or sin and destruction. I remember as a young boy we lived in a town small enough that it was safe for me to walk to other parts of the neighborhood by myself to play with friends. However, the town was also small enough that pretty much everyone knew everyone. My parents would often remind me that just because I was out of their eyesight it didn't mean that someone else was not watching me to see if I was safe and *behaving*. As a matter of fact, I was assured that this *network of watchers* worked so well that if I did misbehave my parents would know about it before I ever stepped foot in our home.

Now I realize that the awareness of being watched did and does help guide my decisions and behavior at various points in my life. Knowing that God is watching helps me keep more of a watch on myself. It's when we quit *watching* our own selves, when we quit being self-aware, that we engage in unhealthy and sinful behavior. When we start making decisions to do things that are harmful to our selves and others we first have to stop *watching*. In other words, at some level of our being we have to turn off that voice of self-awareness that normally would warn us and instead, pretend that what we're doing is really okay. "It won't really lead to the consequences we've been warned to avoid," we tell ourselves. In this state of denial, we suspend the *watching* of our own selves, and pretend that God is not watching either. The results are not pretty. We may initially escape heartaches and pain, but eventually tragedy will most often occur in one form or another.

Ultimately, God is not watching to condemn us. God is watching to invite us to health, wholeness, and deeper relationship with God and one another. The author of Sirach goes on to say, "But the Lord will allow those who repent to return to him. He always gives encouragement to those who are losing hope." In order to repent we must be willing to *watch* our own selves. We must be willing to see, to be self aware, to confront our sin and admit it. Then we must turn to God, fall on divine Grace, and ask the Holy

Wednesday Wonderings

Spirit to help guide us in watching ourselves in the future. I pray that God's Spirit will help me watch *me*. How about you?

72

"... at that very moment ..."

"Jesus gave a command to the demon, and it went out of the boy, and

Wednesday Wonderings

at that very moment he was healed." (Matthew 17:18)

On Father's Day I visited a friend's outdoor model train layout open house. I took a lot of photos and happened to catch this soap bubble that one of the toy trains was popping out as it moved around the track. The bubble lived barely long enough for me to snap this photo. Such beauty, but just for a moment . . .

A moment is not a very long measure of time, but string a few moments together and we get a minute. Put a few more moments together and we have an hour, a few more and we make a day, then keep going until finally a lot of moments linked end on end give us a lifetime. Obviously, lifetimes vary in length yet what each has in common is that at their most elemental level each is a string of moment after moment after moment after moment. In this soap bubble's brief moment of life it reflected beauty and wonder to the eye of the beholder.

One day Jesus met a boy whose life had been plagued by epilepsy. The boy was so plagued by the illness that his seizures often caused him to injure himself by falling into fire or bodies of water. The boy's father brought his son to Jesus to be healed. When the boy met Jesus, Matthew says, "Jesus gave a command to the demon, and it went out of the boy, and at that very moment he was healed." There was a moment in that boy's life, just a moment that turned his life around forever.

Sometimes we get so caught up wondering and worrying about lifetime issues that we miss the moments. A moment can change a lot of things, a lot of relationships, a lot of lives forever. One moment can make the difference between joy and sorrow, hurt and hope, even life and death. Just one simple moment . . .

Sometimes we tell folks, "Don't sweat the small stuff," meaning, don't let your anxiety weigh you down by worrying so much about every little thing. In many circumstances that can be healthy, healing, and freeing advice. However, a healthy respect for moments is also important. A moment can change a life or a relationship, even forever.

The soap bubble I met on Sunday used its moment of life to reflect beauty and wonder. What do we do with our moments? I pray that God will help me have a healthy respect for moments and use each to reflect God's beauty, wonder, and hope. How about you?

73

"... hides ..."

"Insincere talk that hides what you are really thinking is like a fine glaze on a cheap clay pot ... Insincere talk brings nothing but ruin." (Proverbs 26:23 and 28)

Wednesday Wonderings

"Shhhhh! You can't see me. I'm hiding behind this blade of grass!" Someone needs to tell this poor fellow that he's not quite as hidden as he thinks. I really do believe he thought he was hidden because he sat there the entire time, clinging to that blade of grass and allowing me to take several pictures before walking away. Good thing I wasn't a predator, or he'd have been dead meat. His *hiding* reminded me of the times I experience folks *hiding* their true thoughts and feelings in relationships. Instead of honest dialogue they save their real thoughts and harbor them with ill feelings or share them away from the person or persons who really need to hear them.

In church life sometimes we call one version of this the *parking lot meeting after the meeting*. In that particular scenario folks say one thing (or nothing) in the church meeting, then hash over their true thoughts and feelings in the parking lot out of earshot of those who needed to hear. The result is always the same—ill feelings fester and nothing can be accomplished because there can be no real dialogue between the parties who need it while one or both are hiding their true thoughts.

I've watched a similar version of this scenario unfold in personal relationships and marriages. For various reasons individuals decide not to share their true feelings with one another then wonder later why they grow apart and relationships fall into ruin. What do we fear so much about the other that we would risk the ruin of the relationship by not sharing our heart's whispers with them? What could be worse than the ruin of the relationship? Doesn't that kind of thinking seem almost as silly as my damsel fly friend thinking he can hide behind a single blade–of–grass. If we want the relationship, we'd better stop hiding.

This kind of hiding in relationships hurts, pure and simple. That's exactly the wisdom the writer of Proverbs was trying to convey when he said, "Insincere talk brings nothing but ruin." Even our relationship with God is hurt when we hide behind "insincere talk." In that relationship it's not God from whom we hide our true thoughts, feelings, and intentions with insincere talk, but rather, our own selves. Insincere talk with God robs us of the opportunity for true repentance, grace, healing, and transformation.

Hiding hurts and frequently leads to ruin. Sincere and honest dialogue might hurt at first, but often leads to healing. I pray that God will give me the courage in all my relationships not to hide behind *insincere talk*. How about you?

74

". . . judge someone else?"

"God is the only lawgiver and judge. He alone can save and destroy. Who do you think you are, to judge someone else?" (James 4:12)

LAST WEEK WE TOOK our church's youth group for a day of hiking, canoeing, and kayaking. One of the highlights of the hike was this waterfall. Since the water flowed over the edge of a very large rock outcropping it was possible to go behind the falls and get a view through the water from *the other side*.

The view from *the other side of life* is pretty much always different from our own view on our side of the falls. Yet time and again I hear folks express such pain because in the midst of a tragedy or difficult circumstance someone is ready to offer their opinion as seen from their side of the falls as though it's *gospel*. In other words, they're ready to offer that word of judgment based on what they see from their side, but make little or no effort to wonder what the view might be like from the other side of the falls, the back side of the falls.

To wonder what it might be like for the person on the other side of the falls is what we call *empathy*. To walk behind the falls in a situation and attempt to wonder with the hurting person from that perspective can be especially healing, helpful, and hopeful for the one in crisis. That's exactly God's divine agenda, to be with us wherever we find ourselves. However, the word of judgment that is spoken from our side of the falls without the attempt to empathize almost always intensifies the hurt the person in a crisis is already experiencing *behind the falls*.

Judgment rarely, if ever, helps but must serve some purpose or else folks would not be so quick to judge based on the view from their side of the falls. I'm convinced that judgment is a great defense for empathy. To *walk behind the falls* risks our having to encounter our own vulnerability. In other words, it risks our shifting from, "This could *never* happen *to me* . . .." to, "This very well *could* happen to me and it would feel awful. Maybe it would feel so awful that *I* might just make decisions that wouldn't necessarily fit the expected or norm."

To judge means I don't have to feel the pain. I can stay on my side of the falls and you stay on your side. I can pretend that I would never make the sort of decisions you're making in your crisis. It's safe for me, but painful and lonely for you.

James confronts us with, "Who do you think you are, to judge someone else?" I know who I am. I am a vulnerable child of God who has and will again in the future find himself on the *back-side of the falls*. I pray that God will help me remember that so when I see others on the back-side of the falls I can resist judgment and offer hope. How about you?

Wednesday Wonderings

75

". . . sail across dry land . . ."

"Antiochus took 135,000 pounds of silver from the Temple and hurried off to Antioch. Such was his arrogance that he felt he could make ships sail across dry land or troops march across the sea." (II Maccabees 5:21) (An Apocryphal book of the Old Testament.)

Last week I happened on this seed that had unfurled its *sails* and set out across the field I was crossing. What a wondrous spectacle of God's creative genius. The seed sails through the air like a ship through outer space. Unfortunately, its sailing voyage across this field was interrupted by another plant that snagged the *sails* on its seed cone. Because I was also trying to help some folks through relational conflicts this week I was reminded of many life voyages that are interrupted at times by a similar arrogance that wrecked Antiochus when he thought he could, "sail on dry land."

Antiochus was a king known for the conquest of Jerusalem and the slaughter of 40,000 men, women, and children. His arrogance led him to believe he could do anything without suffering repercussions. On the contrary, the Old Testament says his blind arrogance for wealth and power finally led to his undoing and lonely demise. "And so, this murderer, who had cursed God, suffered the same terrible agonies he had brought on others, and then died a miserable death in the mountains of a foreign land." (II Maccabees 9:28)

So, I get it that most of us are not out there arrogantly trying to take over a country. Where I most often experience our arrogance is when we find ourselves in conflict with one another. Like Antiochus, our arrogance frequently leads to the disruptions of our journeys together and painful, lonely suffering. It's normal that we disagree with one another. However, why do we engage in conflicts with that arrogant assurance that we're *completely right*, and the other obviously is *completely wrong*? That one, fatal stance can be the difference between a conflict that results in growth and closeness as we continue to travel together, or a conflict that leads to the end of our journey and the parting of our ways.

"I'm completely right and you're completely wrong," is a defensive posturing that has its roots in hurt and all kinds of fears, including the fear of being hurt again, the fear of being unloved if our weakness is exposed, the fear of feeling inadequate, the fear of not knowing how or being unable to change things about our self that we know are hurtful to others, and more. The arrogance of being right becomes our shield and sword that deceptively keeps us from what we really want and need—relationship with one another.

God's grace (love freely given in spite of our fears, vulnerabilities, weaknesses, etc.) is what we need to save us from our arrogance. If I truly believe that God's grace revealed in Christ for me will hold me *in spite of* that list of my own foibles, then I can take the risk of saying, "Maybe I'm a little right *and* a little wrong, and that leaves a gracious space for you to be both a little wrong *and* a little right." That one careful course correction might just save the voyage we're making together. Arrogance wrecks what only Grace can build. I pray that God will help me steer my course away from arrogance. How about you?

76

"Are any among you . . ."

"Are any among you in trouble? They should pray. Are any among you happy? They should sing praises." (James 5:13)

THIS PAST WEEK PATTI and I spent Wednesday through Sunday with our youth group and about 3500 others from all around the country (and world) at the United Methodist Church's gathering of youth at Purdue University in Indiana. The event was called, "Youth 2011" and will be repeated next week in Sacramento, California for folks on the west coast. The event kicked off with a *bang* (literally—see the pyrotechnics in the photo) and continued with great fellowship, worship, workshops, entertainment, and other special events. The auditorium was thumping and bumping as the crowd rocked with the musicians leading them in worship. Yet . . . I knew a secret . . .

I knew that as I looked out over that sea of faces there were among them those who were "in trouble," as the writer of James put it. They were in trouble because they were suffering from teen depression. As a matter of fact, the statistics tell us that if all the 3500 had been teens, we could have expected that 700 of them would have been suffering from the illness—20 percent. Here's a couple of even more startling numbers. During the time we were together at the festival from noon Wednesday until midnight Saturday over 20,000 young folks in our country in the age range of fifteen to twenty-four attempted suicide. Most of those attempts were fueled by depression. Even worse, by this time next week when Patti and I head to Sacramento for the second half of the Youth 2011 event, one hundred of those young folks who made attempts will have completed suicide and died.

There are those suffering among us, hidden in the crowd of eager, cheerful faces. The truth was further revealed for me after each of the three workshops I taught at Youth 2011 on teen depression. After each workshop there were teens that waited afterward to talk with me and share their stories about their struggles with depression. Some were already getting help and others asked about how they could get help.

I will always especially remember one very tall young man who towered over me. I thought his tears were literally going to drop on me like rain as he shared part of his struggle. Adults also stopped to talk with me at our booth in the exhibit hall. Some of them shared their stories and pain. It helps to know that when you're in the crowd someone knows your secret, someone knows your pain, you're not alone, and there's hope for God's healing.

My workshops really aren't about teen depression. They're really about God's hope and healing. God knows there are those who suffer in our midst—teens and adults—and offers healing. It's time that those who suffer know they need not be the *secret* in the crowd. Depression is an illness like heart disease or diabetes and still has lots of mystery surrounding it; however, depression also has tremendous hope for healing.

In the book of James from the New Testament the author reminds the followers of Christ that their community of faith, their crowd of believers, is composed of folks with various needs and life issues. Some are *happy* and some are *in trouble*. He offers directions for both. We need to be careful and not send a message to those who suffer that tells them they should simply slink into the crowd, pretend to be cheerful, and keep their suffering a secret from the rest of us. That's not the model Jesus offered when he healed the sick.

There is hope, there is healing. That's God's invitation. There are those suffering secretly among us who need to hear that invitation. I pray that God will help me offer that divine invitation to healing and hope. How about you?

77

"... power belongs to him ..."

"Don't put your trust in violence; don't hope to gain anything by robbery; even if your riches increase, don't depend on them. More than once I have heard God say that power belongs to him and that his love is constant." (Psalm 62:10–11)

"... power belongs to him..."

I watched the surfers treading water in the surf near a lighthouse on the California coast. As they paddled around in their wetsuits they really resembled some of the harbor seals bobbing in the water around an outcropping of rocks. Then suddenly, the surfers would spot an approaching wave, paddle to the right spot to catch it, and display some pretty amazing athleticism and acrobatics as they zoomed in and out in front of the twelve-fifteen foot waves behind them. Pretty impressive, yet none of their antics would have been possible were it not for the power of that wall of water that was propelling them.

When times are good we tend to forget the force behind us—the power of God's life-giving love at work for and through us. Unfortunately we risk riding on our own laurels and failing to say thanks to the one whose power truly propels us. When times are bad, our anxiety drives us to seek security and hope in whatever *power* presents itself. That's when we become vulnerable to all kinds of unhealthy and even hurtful schemes.

I learned something from the surfers about power and faith. I watched the surfers long enough to tell you that every wave they rode into shore eventually fizzled out, leaving them beached for a moment and then paddling their way back out to deep water and bobbing around waiting for the next opportunity. I like their discipline. They knew the source of their power. Without the wave, they were nothing more than wet-suited shark bait bobbing in the water. They waited for the wave to come, let the power of the wave direct and flow through them, and then had patience and faith to endure the waiting time for the next big wave. Hmm...

I pray that God will help me practice the discipline of the surfer in my spiritual life—to respond with joy and enthusiasm when I feel the Power of the Spirit at work, and to patiently endure in the *bobbing times*, knowing that the power to propel and hold me in divine love belongs to God whose, "love is constant." How about you?

78

"... grace and peace."

"May God our Father and the Lord Jesus Christ give you grace and peace." (I Corinthians 1:3)

As I stood at the bottom of the spiral staircase and looked up I was keenly aware that my anxiety about high places was escalating to a very un-

". . . grace and peace."

comfortable level. Actually, the anxiety started before I even set foot inside the door of the beautiful lighthouse at Pt. Arena in California. Patti wanted to climb to the top, step out onto the platform around the light, and enjoy the breath-taking view. I wanted to enjoy it as well, so she led the way and we began to scale the spiral stairs toward the top.

By the time we reached the first platform my anxiety had ballooned to a very uncomfortable level. Anxiety like that is strange. It just happens. Some experience it while others are spared. In this case I was really experiencing it, so much so that I told Patti to go ahead without me. I returned to the base of the lighthouse to wait and take pictures.

If Patti or one of my children were in trouble on the top of that lighthouse there is no doubt in my mind that I could and would push through the anxiety and race up the spiral staircase to get to them. As a matter of fact, I have climbed to the top of other lighthouses with my children so that hopefully I would not impart my anxiety of high places to them. However, in this case I decided that the cost of pushing through the anxiety to reach the top was more than I cared to endure for the chance to take a picture from the top. I gave myself a moment of grace. I decided that my *peace* was more important. There was nothing I needed to prove by pushing through this particular bout of anxiety. I kept my feet on the ground and had a great time without any sense of guilt or shame because I didn't push to the top.

Wednesday Wonderings

Anxiety can truly become a problem in life for many people. There have been times in my life when anxiety was such a handicap that I needed relief and healing from a medication. Thank God it was available. If my anxiety ever reached that place again I would not hesitate to ask my physician for medical help. For now, most of my excess anxiety is focused on heights, so I manage it sometimes by pushing through with different techniques (including loud praying, singing hymns, humming, and even shouting) but at other times by making a similar decision to the one I made at the lighthouse—I give myself a moment of grace and in that I find peace.

I'm reminded of the Serenity Prayer when I face these sorts of situations. It says, "God grant me the serenity to accept the things I cannot change; courage to change the things I can; and wisdom to know the difference." I'm not exactly sure which comes first, grace or peace (*serenity*). I think it's really grace. I need God's grace to give me permission to make the best decision I can, and live in peace with myself after I make the decision. It takes both, God's grace and peace. That's why the Apostle Paul offered his blessing, "May God our Father and the Lord Jesus Christ give you grace and peace."

I need the peace that God's grace can bring. I pray that I can live in God's grace and offer it to others. How about you?

79

"... for the good of others..."

"Each one, as a good manager of God's different gifts, must use for the good of others the special gift he has received from God." (I Peter 4:10)

Wednesday Wonderings

ONE FLOWER IS NOTHING short of an intricate, amazing display of God's creative Spirit, but a group of flowers growing together can create a spectacular carpet that just might hint at the glory of heaven!

This Monday morning I walked into our church office, only to be greeted by a message on our answering machine that grated on my nerves. A helpful adult called to let us know that the day before he had been following our church van down the highway and witnessed various pieces of trash (including a milkshake) come tumbling out the back window of our van and scatter on the pavement. It wasn't difficult to locate us since the church name, address, and phone number is painted on the van. I appreciated his call, but couldn't personally thank him because he didn't leave his name or contact info.

You see we are blessed to have (and I mean that seriously) a youth group at this time that is comprised mainly of middle school–age youth. Sunday afternoon we had been traveling with the youth to lunch and then later to our "Under the Bridge" monthly mission trip with the homeless when the trash flew from the van. Developmentally, middle school is a time for youth when a lot of focus is on *me*. They tend to be much more egocentric with a view that it's often okay to do what they want or what their impulses tell them to do as long as they don't get caught. It's much more difficult for them to grasp that they are part of a larger *group* (the human race) and that individual actions have an impact on the *group*.

". . . for the good of others . . ."

I'm not making excuses for their behavior. I'm just trying to name what we're up against as we try to help them learn this critical lesson—namely, that "*me*" is really "*we*" with the *m* turned upside down. In other words, we're trying to help them learn that life is relationship between me, God, and all the other "*me's*." My decisions have an impact on others and vice versa.

That's exactly what the writer of I Peter meant when he admonished the members of the Christian community of faith with, "Each one, as a good manager of God's gifts, must use for the good of others the special gift he has received from God." It is more than a lesson for us to learn. It is a critical transformation necessary for us to live in fellowship with one another and God. Unfortunately I've known some adults who are still awaiting this transformation in their own lives.

Each of us needs to be transformed from *me* to *we* by the awareness of God's love in our lives. This transformation is at the very heart of our individual survival and fulfillment, and also at the very core of our survival as a community, nation, and world. This transformation may come slowly and needs ongoing encouragement and nourishment to be sustained. If we're not careful and attentive it's actually possible to roll the *w* back over and make it *me* again instead of *we*.

Pray for us as we encourage this transformation in our youth. You might want to be in prayer especially this Sunday evening because that's when our youth and leaders will be gathered for fellowship and to listen to that saved message on the church answering machine. I pray that God will give me patience for teaching them, and encouragement for my own ongoing transformation from *me* to *we*. How about you?

80

"... fills us with awe."

"A golden glow is seen in the north, and the glory of God fills us with awe." (Job 37:22)

PATTI AND I WERE driving up the coast of northern California a few weeks ago when suddenly the road veered away from the water and began to wind

". . . fills us with awe."

its way up and up and up and up and up . . . It seemed like there was an endless progression of steep switchbacks with five mph curves as we made our way through dense forests populated by groves of stately redwoods. At the top there was a small pullover along the side of the road. We were gifted with the view in the picture.

Like the Old Testament writer, the glory of God filled us with awe. I think we know it is *awe* when there are no words. Instead, there's that leaping of our soul which wordlessly whispers things like, "Wow," and "Ahhh," or, "Oh Boy!" The feeling of awe is also often accompanied by a feeling of peace and the awareness, like Moses, that we should take off our shoes because we're on holy ground. In other words, we're standing in the presence of God! I felt all those things on the top of that mountain, but I also have to confess that the picture you see at the top is not what I actually viewed. The picture below captures what Patti and I actually saw that day.

If you look carefully you'll be able to see that the top picture is a cropped and enlarged version of a picture like the second one. In other words, we actually got only a glimpse of the spectacular view as the fog rolled over the Pacific Ocean and the redwood forests. The trees were so thick that regardless of how much I paced back and forth, stooping and stretching to see through the limbs, I could catch only a glimpse of the awe-inspiring wonder unfolding below us.

Isn't that often the case—that we catch only a glimpse—a glimpse of the holy, a glimpse of sheer delight, a glimpse of peace, a glimpse of comfort, a glimpse of hope, a glimpse of joy? Yet like Moses who went to the mountaintop and received a glimpse of God face to face, or Martin Luther King, Jr. who said he had been to the mountaintop and seen the Promised Land, we can be inspired and empowered by just that glimpse. We must nurture its memory and act from the encouragement it gives our souls.

A glimpse, just a glimpse, just a moment of awe can change us forever. I pray that God will help me remember the moments when Divine love has awed my soul, and act from them for the sake of God's Kingdom. How about you?

81

"... death..."

"No one can keep from dying or put off the day of death. That is a battle we cannot escape..." (Ecclesiastes 8:8)

THE ERRATIC SWIRLING MOTION in the weeds caught my attention as I walked today. With the telephoto lens on my camera I was able to see that

Wednesday Wonderings

this winged-creature was mired in a spider's web. Just the edge of one wing was stuck, so the creature flapped its wings at hyper-speed, then paused to rest before trying again. I watched it repeat its fruitless efforts for several minutes. It was apparent to me that death was not far around the corner. I even thought about trying to help free the critter, but I figured that if the web was that sticky and powerful, I would probably wind up just further entangling the poor thing. After stopping to change to another lens on my camera I turned around to take a few more photos and was greeted by— the sight of an empty web. This time the little critter had escaped what I thought was to be its certain death. I was wrong . . .

So . . . it got me to thinking . . . How do we know when to move on? How do we know when it's time to bring one chapter of our life to a close and start the next one? How do we know when to struggle against death (or some other change) or accept the inevitable and live graciously into life beyond that death or change?

As a pastor I can remember being confronted by that question many times when I've walked the journey of terminal illness or some other crisis with others. I can still see the faces of those who've asked, "When do I fight? How long do I fight? Is it ever okay not to fight? When is it okay to accept the end? Am I a *quitter* if I stop fighting and get ready for the next chapter of my life?" These are important questions we all face from time to time during many different kinds of crises in our lives. The crisis might be a severe illness or it might also be a difficult time in a relationship.

Obviously, the little critter I met today knew that it was time to fight, so it fought mightily and won. How do we know? Can someone else know for us? I guess that's what I have come to know over time—that I can't know for someone else. I know that it is important for us to reach a point in some crisis in our lives where we move from fighting to continue one chapter into closing it and moving on to the next. However, I don't think I can tell someone else when they've reached that time, even if the person desperately wants me to make that decision for them. I can only walk with them as they discern that transition point with God. I can let them know that there are times when it's important to fight. I can also let them know that it's okay to reach the awareness that it's time to start a new chapter.

I can assure them that after prayerful discernment with God writing a new chapter is not *quitting* or *giving up*, but I can't tell them when that moment has arrived for them. That's a very sacred moment between an individual and God. Once the decision is made they have to be able to trust it. The only way to trust that decision is to know it is *their* decision borne out of prayer and wrestling with God, not simply the opinion offered by a well-meaning friend. Besides, look at today. I got it wrong. I was certain that little critter was buzzing away its last few moments of life.

I pray that God will help me discern the moments for my transitions—when to fight, and when to accept change—when to stay, and when to move on. I also pray that God will give me the wisdom, patience, and grace to walk with others through their crises and transitions. How about you?

82

"... imitate ..."

"My dear friend, do not imitate what is bad, but imitate what is good. Whoever does good belongs to God; whoever does what is bad has not seen God." (III John 1:11)

"... imitate ..."

THIS WEEK PATTI AND I are leading a group from our church on an adventure in Washington, D.C. and the surrounding area. We began our trip Monday with a visit to Pohick Episcopal Church (the church George Washington attended and served as a vestryman), moved on to Mt. Vernon, and ended the day with a picnic at a small park with a pretty amazing location. The park is situated right at the end of the runway of Reagan National Airport. We ate our pizza as we watched the jets take off so close to the top of our heads that we were sure the pilots could look down and tell if we were eating plain cheese or pepperoni and cheese pizza.

We were separated from the end of the runway by a very small inlet from the river, where several ducks plied the waters and scrambled onto the banks trying to seduce picnickers into feeding them. Suddenly a new guy flew into the gathering of ducks near us, maneuvering like the planes overhead to get his *flaps* in position and his *landing gear* up or down as needed for the landing or take offs. "Look at me," he seemed to say, "I can do that too," as he tried to steal the show from the planes overhead.

Today I stood in the gallery dedicated to the work of the Wright brothers at the Smithsonian's Air and Space Museum. As I walked around the large room I admired their airplane that made the first powered flight and was the centerpiece of the display. However, I also was struck by the fact that the curators had taken care to tell the story of how the Wright brothers had made their historic flight by imitating and building upon the earlier research and findings of others. My thoughts returned to that little duck I'd seen coming in for a landing. Look at the two photos one more time. Hmm, wings... landing gear... Looks like I can fly across the country in a jetliner because a whole lot of folks learned how to imitate a duck.

There's so much to be learned from imitating and building upon a healthy model, and so much to be lost from imitating the bad ones. It is such a simple principle, but one that we seem to quickly ignore if it suits our fancy. As Christians we are called to imitate Christ so that others might see Christ in us and also want to imitate what they see.

I don't know about the rest of you, but I know that sometimes I get tired of being a role model. There are times when I just want to not have to care that others might be watching me to see if they can gain something from the Christ in me that they need and want to imitate. I guess those times when I'm tired are the times when I most need to be on my guard and remind myself that people really are watching.

I give thanks to God for those in whom I've seen Christ and watched so I could imitate. I pray that God will give me strength, patience, and perseverance so others will see Christ in me and want to imitate that Divine Love. How about you?

83

"... surprised ..."

"At that moment Jesus' disciples returned, and they were greatly surprised to find him talking with a woman." (John 4:27)

I WAS WALKING THROUGH the National Botanical Gardens last week and was surprised by this one lonely blossom shooting from the cactus plant draped over the rocks. That's one of the reasons I'm fond of cacti. The plants are bizarre and beautiful, but then almost out of nowhere come these amazingly gorgeous blossoms. What a surprise!

Sometimes surprise brings delight and joy, while other times it brings heartache and pain. I've been surprised by the goodness and generosity of some, and surprised by the rudeness and callousness of others. What do we do when we're surprised? A surprise can be a pivotal moment in a relationship. How we respond might just make a difference between our being drawn closer together, or our being pushed further apart.

When Jesus surprised the disciples they responded by respectfully listening and learning. They grew in their relationship with Jesus and each other. So . . . if how we respond to a surprise can be so important, what are we to do? We can't plan for a surprise, can we? Maybe we can't plan, but can we prepare? Yes, I believe we can. If we practice appreciation and giving thanks, then I think when surprised by beauty, kindness, or generosity we will be more likely to pause and notice the surprise and acknowledge with thanksgiving and joy. If we practice patience, humility, and forgiveness, then I think when surprised by rudeness and callousness we are more likely to respond with grace rather than retaliation.

We can't plan, but we can prepare. That's exactly what Jesus was doing with disciples—preparing them for all the surprises they would encounter as they lived out the Kingdom's message of peace, hope, and love. I pray that God will help me prepare. How about you?

84

"... invisible ..."

"Ever since God created the world, his invisible qualities, both his eternal power and his divine nature, have been clearly seen; they are perceived in the things that God has made." (Romans 1:20)

BELIEVE IT OR NOT, this is a picture of a woman standing in front of the old courthouse building in colonial Williamsburg, VA. More accurately, this is a picture of a woman dressed in a colonial dress and hat walking from the right side of the picture and stopping at the front door. She's carrying a lantern with a candle burning inside.

The picture was created a little differently than most. The street was in almost total darkness when the picture was taken. The camera was sitting on a tripod to keep it steady while the shutter was allowed to stay open for about five seconds, just enough time for the woman to come from around the right side of the building and walk in front of my camera. The photo is not *doctored* or *photo-shopped* in any way. What you see in the photo is exactly what the camera saw in the darkness. The evidence of the woman's presence is clear in the bright trail of light from her lantern, even though the rest of her is invisible. I was amazed when I saw the finished photo.

I agree with Paul when he wrote in Romans that God's, "invisible qualities, both his eternal power and his divine nature, have been clearly seen; they are perceived in the things that God has made." The woman in the photo is invisible but her presence is indisputable in the brightness of the light she carries. Sometimes I find myself too focused on what I can't see—like the solution to a problem, the outcome of some dilemma, or the reason for some confusion or hurt. That sort of focus can lead to more confusion, frustration, and even doubt. If I remain focused on what I can't see for too long, then eventually the questions might even become, "So where is God in all of this anyway?" or "Does God even care?" or "Does God even exist?"

Especially in those difficult times I find the need to pull my focus back to what I can see—the evidence of God's presence in the miracles around me—the beauty of creation and the wonder of shared love. I can't see the woman in the photo but I can sure see her light! She's really there, no doubt about it! That light didn't move by itself. I may not be able to see the outcome to my present dilemma, but I can see the hand of God at work in so many other ways and times in my life.

There is a lot of God's presence to be known and shared if we focus more on what we can see instead of what we can't see. I pray that God will remind me to look for the presence of divine love all around me. How about you?

85

"... unyielding ..."

I knew that you would prove to be stubborn, as rigid as iron and unyielding as bronze." (Isaiah 48:4)

A COUPLE OF WEEKS ago we were in Yorktown, Virginia and stopped to visit Grace Episcopal Church in the middle of the historic town. The parish dates its origins to 1634 and the construction of its first building in 1697. I'm told that the current church was rebuilt on the same site in 1920 along with the wall you see in the picture. I was amazed when I saw this tree. I looked and looked but could not figure out if the wall was built around the tree or if the tree somehow engulfed the wall. (I called the church to ask about the tree but they weren't sure about its origins.) One thing that is evident is that this tree is stubborn and unyielding. Regardless of its origins the tree has stood its ground and engulfed this wall.

Sometimes stubbornness and unyieldingness are positive traits expressing the certitude and fortitude necessary to make or keep a stand. In a key battle a general wants troops that are stubborn and unyielding. In some situations a stubborn and unyielding faith is necessary to survive hardship and crisis. Surely the stubbornness and unyieldingness of this tree has helped ensure its survival.

However, in the book of Isaiah, the Lord was not complimenting the Israelites when they were called, "stubborn, as rigid as iron and unyielding as bronze." In this case the Israelites were being called to task because they were too stubborn and rigid to see and admit they were headed down the wrong path. Their stubbornness, rigidity, and unyieldingness were setting them up for more pain and sorrow. They could not stop, really listen, admit they're mistake, seek forgiveness, and change course. Instead, they insisted they were right and destroyed their relationship with God and their very lives.

I've met a few of those folks. Even when they discover that they're wrong they cling to their point. Is it shame that they invested so much of themselves in the issue only to be proven wrong that keeps them lashed to a lie? Is it fear of embarrassment? Sometimes it takes more courage and grace to admit error than it does to stand stubbornly and unyieldingly on a false premise.

God's grace invites us to respond with honesty, and offers healing and hope in return. I pray for God's wisdom to know when to stand unyieldingly and when to admit I'm wrong and ask for grace. How about you?

86

"... turn back ..."

"We are not people who turn back and are lost. Instead, we have faith and are saved." (Hebrews 10:39)

Does it . . .? Are you certain . . .? How do you know . . .?

Wednesday Wonderings

If you were driving through our community this morning and decided to head across this bridge that spans the Ohio River, would you have continued across the river or turned back for fear that there was no end to the bridge on the other side? Sounds like a pretty dumb question, doesn't it? I think 99.999 per cent of us would have continued to drive right across to the other side. But why would we have made that decision? From this angle it does look a little daunting, doesn't it? Is there an end? What's at the end? What would have given us the confidence to continue?

Why would you have continued to drive across the bridge? Might it have been because you had driven across many other bridges similar to this one and always found your way to the other side of the river? Might it have been because after you started to drive across the bridge you realized that with each yard you drove you were able to see another yard into the distance? Often we move right on through the moment and don't even stop to think about all the previous experiences that have given us the confidence to face the fog.

Sometimes we face situations that may make us feel like we're on a bridge that seems to have no end—or at least an end that we cannot see, and suddenly we're not sure about the end. I've been on a few of those bridges and felt the urge to stop or turn around. In those times God has reminded me of the other bridges we've crossed together. In those times God has also urged me to take another step and see that the fog is clearing enough to see the way to the next step. Facing the next unknown through the fog is not necessarily as daunting as it may seem if we remember that we've been on similar bridges in life and God has gotten us through.

The writer of Hebrews reminds us that we are not to be, "people who turn back and are lost." Instead, we have faith, keep moving, and are saved by God's abiding love. I pray that God will help me keep moving over the bridge. How about you?

87

"... bar your way..."

"The angel demanded, 'Why have you beaten your donkey three times like this? I have come to bar your way, because you should not be making this journey.'" (Numbers 22:32)

Wednesday Wonderings

WE WERE TREKKING DOWN a major highway in southern West Virginia last week when I saw this sign just off to the right on a side road. Immediately I found the next place to turn around and went back to get this picture. You just don't see many signs like this. Now, if that sign wouldn't stop you I don't know what would. We can get so caught up in our emotions and irrational thinking at times that we need a roadblock to keep us from barreling down a road to our own destruction and the ruin of others. Sometimes we need to have our way barred.

In the story from the book of Numbers in the Old Testament the angel of the Lord tries three times to get Balaam's attention through the faltering of his donkey. Instead of standing back and wondering why in the world a faithful and hardworking donkey would suddenly falter, Balaam gets lost in his frustration and beats the poor animal not once, but three times. Finally the angel of the Lord has to bar his way to get Balaam to come to his senses.

In the early days of our teen-age son's journey through terrible depression and anxiety he began to miss more and more school. Suddenly this great, honor-roll student would simply stare at me from his bed in the morning when I went into his room to awaken him and say, "I just can't go to school." I would then proceed to get angry and verbally *push* him to go—all to no avail. With each repetition of this drama I found myself getting angrier and angrier, until I could feel myself so angry that I wanted to pick him up and throw him through the wall. My anger finally intensified to the point that as soon as he said, "I can't go," I wheeled around and went back upstairs before I had a chance to do something stupid and tragic.

The drama with my son continued until one day the Lord barred my way. I felt the Spirit of the Lord stop me in my tracks and the following dialogue occurred:

Spirit of the Lord: "Gary, what in the world do you think you're doing? You're yelling at this child you cherish because he's ill? Listen to yourself!" What are you afraid of?"

Gary: (And that's when it hit me that my anger was being fueled by my fear and helplessness.) "I'm afraid! I'm afraid my son won't get back to school. I'm afraid he'll fail. I'm afraid he won't graduate. I'm afraid he won't have a life. I'm afraid others will find out and no one will come to me for counseling. Then I'm afraid that I won't be able to support my family. And then I'm afraid . . . "

Spirit of the Lord: "Gary, I've got this. Give me your fear and your helplessness, and you just keep loving your son."

"... *bar your way* ..."

That's when I felt the anger melt away, and from that day on I was able to keep a healthy relationship with our son that was healing instead of destructive. Oh, I slipped now and then after that, but each time I heard the Spirit of the Lord saying, "Gary, remember, just keep loving him," and I got back on track. It took the Lord blocking my way that fateful day to keep me from going further down a path of irrational anger that could have destroyed so much. I pray that if necessary in the future, God will bar my way and set me back on God's way. How about you?

88

"... predict the weather..."

"Hypocrites! You can look at the earth and the sky and predict the weather; why, then, don't you know the meaning of this present time?" (Luke 12:56)

"... predict the weather..."

SOMETIMES I FEEL SORRY for the weather prognosticators. Not fifteen minutes before I took this picture of a farm in northern Illinois near Chicago last week Patti and I watched a ferocious snowstorm viciously whip across the seemingly endless level cornfields. Then, *presto*, clear skies and a gorgeous moon! I can't imagine what the weather forecasters were saying about all of that. You know the joke, "If you really want to know what the weather's going to be you better stick your head outside and look!" In this case that would have been the most accurate way to predict what we experienced. However, the truth is the weather forecasters have very sophisticated instruments, models, etc. that do allow them to make some amazingly accurate weather predictions from what they see. When they look at their data they are often able to give us a very good picture of what will happen weather-wise so we can adjust our lives accordingly.

In this scripture passage from the Gospel of Luke Jesus was confronting the people because they could look at physical signs around them and make accurate predictions of the weather, but they refused to see what was right in front of them—God's amazing love for them at work in the person of Jesus. Unfortunately we *are* capable of choosing *not to see* what we *do see*, even if it's right in front of us. Sometimes we choose not to see because we're so startled by what's in front of us that we're not sure we can really *believe our eyes*. It can be so difficult to make it fit into our concept of reality that we finally choose to say to ourselves and others, "I must have been mistaken. Surely I didn't really see what I thought I saw." "I know this person," we tell ourselves, "and the person I know would never do what I think I just saw. Surely what the other person said they saw or what I thought I saw was impossible."

Because we can't make what we see make sense with what we think we know we decide we really didn't see what we saw. Maybe we decide not to see because we're afraid of the consequences of seeing. If we admit we see something then it might force us to have to act upon what we see and that might turn our lives and the lives of others upside down. Maybe we're not sure we can risk the ramifications of seeing. Not admitting what we see can have dire and dangerous consequences.

I write this as the Penn State scandal continues to unfold. I do not presume to know whether the alleged perpetrator is guilty or innocent of the heinous crimes he is accused of having committed. However, I do know from many years of listening to the terrifying stories of sexual abuse victims that in many cases the victim knew that folks in their lives saw what was happening to them but chose not to see. The consequences of others not seeing (and thus acting) resulted in even more pain and suffering. In the Gospel of Luke Jesus is confronting the people because he knows they can see the power of God at work in Him, but yet, they refuse to acknowledge what they see. Their chosen blindness will have consequences.

We must have the courage and faith to acknowledge what we see. I know there are times when we can be mistaken. However, I think in our culture today we err too often on the side of not acknowledging what we see because of the reasons I've named and more. If it comes to the safety of a child or adult we need to check out what we see and let others help us decide whether or not we really saw what we thought we saw. Choosing not to see what we saw without checking it further can have dire and dangerous consequences.

I pray that God will give me the courage and faith to see. How about you?

89

"... my heart is like melted wax."

"My strength is gone, gone like water spilled on the ground. All my bones are out of joint; my heart is like melted wax." (Psalm 22:14)

THIS PAST SATURDAY A very *happy pappy* brought this beauty to our church's Fall Festival. It was, by far, the snappiest, coolest, hottest, hippest, gnarliest, raddist, dandiest, smartest, slickest, neatest, smoothest, most outrageous and bodacious beast of burden in the parking lot that day. This pickup truck is so amazing and old that it takes several decades worth of superlatives to describe it. I could tell its owner was having a lot of fun with his *big green toy*.

There are a lot of things that give us pleasure and help us enjoy life to its fullest. What are some of the things that do it for you? As you can probably surmise, photography has become a lot of fun for me, right up at the top along with banging on my drums and making music with others. I also enjoy traveling with my wife and riding roller coasters with our family. Isn't it great that God created us to enjoy so many of the fruits of divine creation?

Yet sometimes folks will find themselves feeling like the psalmist, "my heart is like melted wax." It's almost as though all the things that used to be fun and fulfilling are meaningless now. It feels like they're just going through the motions of living. They could be doing their favorite activity with their favorite person and just feel *blah*, or *so what*? They no longer feel like playing with their *toys*. Sure, we all have a day or two now and then when we might feel like the psalmist, but when that feeling lasts for weeks or months (or years) instead of days, we call it clinical depression.

The technical word for this particular symptom of depression is "anhedonia," the inability to feel pleasure. This anhedonia is also frequently accompanied by a spiritual crisis—the person may not feel pleasure, but they may also report that they cannot feel God. This can frighten them into thinking that they've, "lost their faith," or even worse, "that God has abandoned them."

Nothing could be further from the truth. We all have times in our spiritual journeys when we feel closer to God, more inspired by God, or more excited by God than other times. But this anhedonia can make a person feel like they've lost God. Psalm 22 is a powerful writing that portrays one of the best descriptions of depression I've ever read. The psalmist pours their heart out with frustration, anger, and pain. However, the psalm ends with an important twist. In the midst of the pain the psalmist remembers what God has done in the past and therefore proclaims that God can bring healing in the future.

There is healing for depression. If you are afflicted with the illness, know that God has not abandoned you. God can heal through many different means. Consult professionals who can point you in the right direction for that healing. Don't keep your pain a secret. I pray that God will help me point the suffering toward the divine healing available. How about you?

90

"What right do you have . . ."

". . . As Jesus was walking in the Temple, the chief priests, the teachers of the Law, and the elders came to him and asked him, 'What right do you have to do these things? Who gave you such right?'" (Mark 11:27–28)

Wednesday Wonderings

BOOM! RIGHT IN YOUR face! Forgive me. I know it's a cannon, actually one from a civil war battlefield. I offer it not so much because it's a cannon but rather for the feel of the picture. Doesn't it give you sort of an, *in your face* feeling and almost make you want to recoil backwards from it? You know what I mean, don't you? Your moving along in a relationship or situation and then suddenly, almost out of the blue, someone lands the *in your face explosion* and you're left wondering, "Well now what do I say?" You can feel the sudden shift in the winds from the rational to the irrational. That's why there's that sense of, "What in the world just happened?" or "How do we move on from here?" or "Well, that's the end of that effort to communicate with them . . ."

I've learned to call this sort of posturing the offensive defense. It's a very aggressive form of defense, something akin to the bite of an injured dog offered when someone attempts to approach and help. The *in your face* response in a relationship often arises from a sense of fear on the part of the aggressor. Once it happens, it leaves us in about the same position as the one trying to help the injured dog—we stop our efforts and reassess whether we can continue or just need to back away. *In your face* sort of comments and remarks tend to destroy relationships.

I'm convinced that on the day when the chief priests and others met Jesus in the Temple they had already heard enough about him to be frightened. He was rocking their boat and their world. When they met him, they weren't looking to dialogue and build a relationship. They were looking to shut him down. "Who gave you such right? There, in your face—take that—let's see you come back from that one! That'll shut you down!" and unspoken, "Then we'll be safe again." Fear, when shoved into the face of the other, is always dangerous for the relationship.

From the rest of the dialogue I gather that when Jesus responded it was not in kind. In other words, he didn't respond with, "Oh yeah, well here's one in your face. Right back at you!" His more thoughtful response required him to check the visceral emotions that *in your face* arouses in the one verbally slapped, pause for a moment, and respond from the rational instead of the irrational. In doing so Jesus actually offered the possibility for the chief priests and others to change course and build relationship. Obviously, they chose not to, but Jesus provided the possibility in the way that he responded.

I find it can be difficult not to respond in kind. When someone shoves their fear in my face and I recoil, feelings well up and make me want to protect myself. Sometimes I think it would feel so good to shove that fear right back into their face, but the results would not be pretty, productive, or grace–filled. It might feel good in the moment, but the results would be disastrous for the relationship. An *in your face* response on my part certainly would not be a loving gesture. Recognizing what just got shoved in my face (fear) can help me pause and consider my next move. Then hopefully I can offer grace and the possibility for relationship to continue. Hopefully, I can respond to fear with love.

I pray that God will help me avoid shoving my fear into someone's face, and have the insight and discipline to offer grace when their fear gets shoved into mine. How about you?

91

"... follow their instructions..."

**"Accept their verdict and follow their instructions in every detail."
(Deuteronomy 17:11)**

OKAY, SO YOU THINK it's so amazing that one of our Boston Terriers is reading the instructions for the new Christmas toy before attempting to demolish it. A lot of folks would say the truly amazing thing is that it's our *male* Boston terrier reading the instructions before attempting to demolish it. Sorry for that one guys, but let's face it, we're often the ones found

". . . follow their instructions . . ."

guilty of trying to assemble all those Christmas morning toys on Christmas Eve without first reading the instructions. Why won't Tab C fit into Slot C? Oops, it's because we were supposed to attach Flap A before attempting that Tab C to Slot C step. Guessed we missed that one. You get my drift.

I remember early in my ministry I decided to make homemade bread from scratch. I dumped in all the ingredients and wound up with pretty good tasting, but very, very flat bread. An expert bread maker listening to my lament informed me that my bread didn't rise because I failed to follow the instructions about the order of adding the ingredients, and subsequently killed the yeast before it had a chance to make the bread rise.

Trust me, it's not just us men who are guilty of setting the instructions aside and doing it our way, or skipping a few steps that we deem unnecessary for our situation. I can tell you several occasions where folks (male and female) would ask for my help, leave my office with a pretty clear set of instructions about what might prove helpful (and had been helpful for others), only to return frustrated and upset by their failure. When I asked them if they had followed all the things on the list they responded, "Well, I did the first and third thing you said, but I didn't do the second and fourth thing."

Why do we ask for help if we're not willing to follow the instructions of the ones we trust enough to ask? Is it because we think we know ourselves better than the one we're asking so obviously we can take their instructions as sort of mere *guidelines* to be amended as we deem fit? Is it because we're too scared to follow the instructions because we're afraid we'll still fail and then not have a fall back excuse? Is it because we're misinformed and decide to follow the advice of the many instead of the trusted one we've asked? Is it because we've been hurt before and we're just too scared to really trust? Is it because we just don't want to *waste* the time to do something we deem unnecessary? Is it because we're always looking for the shortcut or quick and easy fix after having been trained by a *quick-fix* culture? Is it because we can't see the reason for the instruction so we dismiss it without risking following it until we *can* see an outcome? Is it because_____?

Please don't get the idea that I'm suggesting we blindly follow without thinking and evaluating the instructions we've been offered. It is critical that our faith and decision-making be informed and guided by rigorous evaluating, reasoning, and questioning. However, it seems to me that all too often we are quick to dismiss the wisdom that might be behind the instructions that have been offered to us. Why waste time, just dump in all the bread ingredients at once . . .

This is not something new. I suspect this has been the same for ages, thus prompting God's warning to the Israelites in the passage from Deuteronomy. The problem is not new and neither is the result—more pain.

As I travel through Advent this year I am keenly aware that Christmas is a celebration of the wondrous Divine gift of relationship with God and one another that comes through Christ—and comes with instructions. Step 1: Love God. Step 2: Love One Another. They're simple instructions, but ones without shortcuts, even though many have tried—and failed to find the shortcuts. I want to enjoy the gift of relationship that God's wisdom offers.

I pray that God will help me not to allow any one or more of my excuses to get in the way of following these simple instructions. I pray that God will help me trust in Divine Wisdom. How about you?

92

"... and light appeared..."

"In the beginning, when God created the universe, the earth was formless and desolate. The raging ocean that covered everything was engulfed in total darkness, and the Spirit of God was moving over the water. Then God commanded, 'Let there be light' — and light appeared. God was pleased with what he saw." (Genesis 1:1-3)

Wednesday Wonderings

Across the river from our community is the town of Marietta, Ohio. Its levee on the river has long been the landing site for many famous sternwheelers over the centuries. Makes sense that part of their Christmas decorations would include a festive light display in the shape of a sternwheeler. The waters of the Ohio River on a dark and cloudy night are generally black and ominous, but with the lights of the Christmas display shining down a spectacular mosaic of light is reflected. What a show!

Last evening as I walked across the lawn from our home to the church there was a loud pop and several street lights went out. I guess a nearby transformer blew. Suddenly I was very aware of just how dark our neighborhood really is without the lights on the nearby poles. Most of the time I'm insulated from the darkness by the warm light from above. The experience reminded me of just how close we are to darkness in our lives—maybe just a blown transfer away, maybe a heartbeat away, maybe a sudden crisis away, or even a memory away—from darkness.

In reality it does not take that much for us to find ourselves in the midst of a moment (or the memory of a moment) where life begins to feel as though the waters are closing around us until total darkness threatens to envelop us. I am aware that for many the Christmas season brings with it a certain amount of darkness. Memories of painful or lost relationships, economic stress flamed by a manic spending culture, loneliness and more give rise to the darkness.

What keeps the darkness from totally enveloping us? Every time I strike a match I'm reminded of the miracle of light and what it is required to call it forth. I can strike a match or flip a switch, but I can't call forth light. I can't stand by myself against the darkness without help, and if I try on my own for too long, the darkness might envelop and convince me it has won. Only the Spirit of God can move across the darkness of the water and say, "Let there be light!" When that Light is allowed to shine in our darkness, our lives can reflect the mosaic of hope and peace. It's never too late!

Christmas is a celebration of the Spirit of God once more moving over the waters of our darkness and saying, "Let there be Light." This time God's Light comes in the flesh with the birth of Jesus. Like the murky waters of the Ohio gleaming with the light from the Christmas display, the Divine Light can transform the darkness of our lives and world. As I celebrate the birth of Jesus Christ this Christmas, I pray that God will help me seek the Light, bear the Light, and share the Light. How about you?

93

"... too lazy to plow ..."

"A farmer too lazy to plow his fields at the right time will have nothing to harvest." (Proverbs 20:4)

This New Year's Day was a tough time to be a tugboat captain on the river. As I took this photo I only could imagine the frustration of the captain and pilot. They were fighting to keep their coal–laden barges on course in the channel as they plowed through the fierce winds and waves. I guess they knew their coal had to get to market so they struggled on instead of

Wednesday Wonderings

waiting out the storm. Sometimes life does present us with situations where our only recourse is to just plow right on through—but do we?

When I hear about the *lazy farmer* in the Proverb at first I want to use that favorite teen phrase, "Well duhhhh . . ." In other words, it seems like such a *no-brainer* to realize that if you don't plow your field and plant your crop there won't be any crops to harvest. Why would anyone need to say such a thing? Why would anyone have to be reminded of something that seems like the most basic common sense? Maybe it's because sometimes there are those who find themselves not "plowing their field" when they should be, knowing full well that their lack of action means there will be no *crops*. Why would anyone not do something that they know later will cause them heartache, suffering, and misery? Hmm . . . I guess they must be lazy?

The writer of Proverbs is trying to point out that something must be wrong with a person who would intentionally neglect something while knowing it could mean life or death for their family. I think the writer's point is not to simply judge the person by calling them *lazy*, but rather, to lift up alarm that something is dreadfully wrong and in need of attention. Maybe in those days the only word they had to describe such a person was, *lazy*. Today I still hear that word used a lot, but in many if not most cases there is a better word—"depressed."

Clinical depression can often look like *laziness*. The person knows what they need to do, what they have to do, what they better do, but they just can't bring themselves to do it. Maybe they feel overwhelmed by difficult and even not so difficult tasks. Maybe they feel so fatigued that they can't pick themselves up and perform even simple things, let alone plow through a difficult life experience. When a person is not doing something they know will later result in more pain and suffering for them it means there really is something wrong. The writer of Proverbs is right about that. However, today I think we can give it a different name—"clinical depression," and hopefully point the person in the direction of the help they need so they eventually can get back to *plowing their field*.

It is easy for us to judge the other and say, "They're just lazy." It requires more energy, insight, patience, and prayer for us instead to offer a moment of grace and wonder *why* the person might be struggling with something that seems so self-evident, necessary, important, and common sense. That grace–filled moment when we resist the urge to judge and instead *wonder about their situation in effort to understand* might be the first

"... *too lazy to plow* ..."

step that person needs toward the healing and hope God has to offer for a fierce illness like depression.

I pray that God will help me *wonder* in a moment of grace and offer an invitation for healing instead of another helping of judgmental beating.

How about you?

94

"... will be your eternal light..."

"No longer will the sun be your light by day or the moon be your light by night; I, the Lord, will be your eternal light; The light of my glory will shine on you." (Isaiah 60:19)

I GOT OUT OF the car and turned to go in a shop with my family when I glanced up the hill and saw this old cemetery. I was immediately drawn to

"... *will be your eternal light* ..."

something. It took a moment for me to realize that it was the light calling me. The day was ending, just a few minutes before sunset, and the light reflecting upon the tombstones on top of the hill against an angry winter sky was especially magnificent.

Since starting to take more photos I've discovered that I've become increasingly sensitive to light. There's light—and then there's light . . . Patti, my wife, would confirm that on many occasions as we've been driving down the highway she's heard me remark, "Wow, look at that light!" I think the same can be said for our spiritual relationship with God. There's God—and then there's God . . .

Our spiritual connection with God changes as we deliberately focus more of our attention on God. There's God—the distant, "I guess I'd better behave or else God will get me" God—and then there's God—the intimate spiritual companion on our journey who listens to our joys and sorrows reminding us, "I the Lord, will be your eternal light . . ." God is always the same, but it's our attention to the relationship that develops it into a more intimate experience. In that experience we come to know the wonder, majesty, support, and challenge of the one who promises to offer a very special Light—the Light of divine glory—the Light of eternity.

I pray that God will help me focus more attention on our relationship through prayerful dialogue, study, worship, and fellowship with my fellow travelers. How about you?

95

"... misled by their own opinions ..."

"Many people have been misled by their own opinions; their wrong ideas have warped their judgment." (Sirach 3:23-25) (An Apocryphal book of the Old Testament)

"... *misled by their own opinions* ..."

THERE ARE ALWAYS TWO sides—or maybe three or more! How quickly I learned that as a young pastor when I was starting out in my career. There were several occasions when someone would share with me a very harsh description of another person or situation. The picture I got of the person was not very flattering. Later, when I had a chance to listen to the other person's side of the story, the picture sometimes (but not always) changed rather dramatically. There were even a few times when I was especially grateful that I didn't act before hearing the other side of the story. Had I jumped to an opinion and acted based on only the first story I heard I might have added even more hurt and confusion to the situation.

Last Friday and Saturday I was speaking at a youth retreat in southern New Jersey. On our way to the retreat we made a quick trip over to the shore where I took the photo *above* looking from the east as the sun was setting on Barnegat Lighthouse. Barely five minutes earlier I took the photo *below* of the same lighthouse looking from the west.

What a difference it made to walk around the lighthouse tower and view it from the other side! I've discovered that it's always important to *walk around the tower* to avoid being misled by my own ill-informed opinions and warped judgments. Whether it's another side to a story offered by a second party or a problem that needs an approach from a different

Wednesday Wonderings

perspective, that *walk around the tower* (as I'll forever come to call it after these photos) is critical.

A *walk around the tower* also provides us the opportunity to invite God into the process through prayerful reflection and discernment. *Walking* provides not only a different perspective, but also the opportunity to remember that we need not face and make decisions alone. Whew!!!

I pray that God will remind me to always *walk around the tower*. How about you?

96

"... poured out his abundant grace..."

"And our Lord poured out his abundant grace on me and gave me the faith and love which are ours in union with Christ Jesus." (I Timothy 1:14)

Wednesday Wonderings

AT THE END OF last summer my string trimmer overheated and stubbornly refused to let me finish cutting the rest of the tall weeds on the steep hillside beside my house. Before I could get the trimmer fixed fall morphed into winter and the weeds remained. (I've still got to get the trimmer fixed.) The weeds don't really bother me that much but it bothers me knowing that it probably bothers others. Last week we had a pretty decent ice storm that transformed the weeds into a work of art. I was busy during the day and didn't get the opportunity to take many photos, so I went outside after dark and snapped the one above with a long exposure and a little help from the garage light reflecting on the hillside. The ugliness from my neglect was transformed into a strange sort of beauty by God's covering it with shimmering ice.

When we contemplate our *sins* we usually focus more on the things we've done that need forgiveness. Often I find that it's the things I've left undone that cause me the most grief—my sins of omission. I think of the things I could have done as a pastor—all the visits I could have made, the phone calls I could have made, the extra sermon preparation time I could have spent . . . If I let myself I can even go further with it and think of all the things I might have done as a father, a husband, a son, a brother, a friend.

Oh, trust me, I contemplate the hurtful things I've done and ask forgiveness, but I really think that it's often the things I feel I've left undone that cause me the most pain and seem so ugly. So . . . I see these weeds, one example of my *undone sins* that God has transformed, and I think, "Yes, it's true . . . God's grace can cover all my sins—even the *undone*—my sins of omission." Once more I feel the relief, peace, and hope of this grace that keeps me from getting stuck in my regret. God's grace can cover—just ask.

I pray that God will remind me of divine grace when I find my self stuck on my *undone*. How about you?

97

"... he was lost ..."

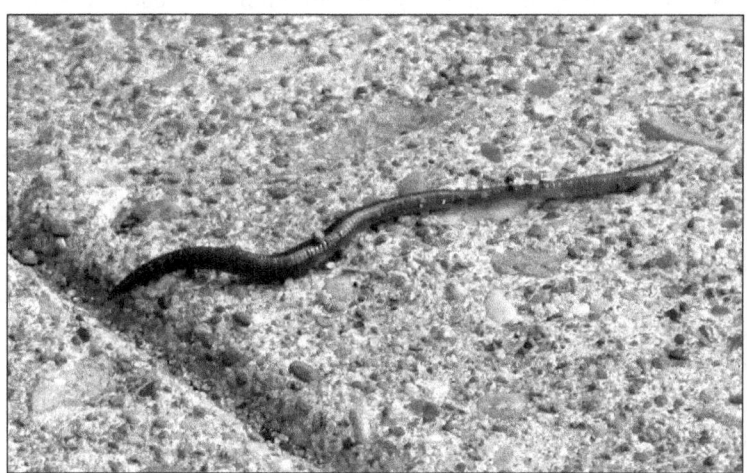

"For this son of mine was dead, but now he is alive; he was lost, but now he has been found." (Luke 15:24)

So, WHY DID THE chicken cross the road? Better yet, today I ask, "Why did the *earthworm* cross the sidewalk—when he could have stayed in the relative safety of the grass and earth where he belonged?" I was plagued by this deep philosophical question this morning as I emerged from our clergy coffee group only to find this guy in the photo struggling across the sidewalk and headed toward the parking lot. From the looks of him you can already tell he was doomed. He was dehydrated with the beginnings of that classic shriveled-up, dry, almost-dead-on-the-concrete look about him. Pieces of rock had already started to stick to his skin—and yet, he continued to head away from the earth and grass that might have saved him and toward the black asphalt that would have cooked him in just a few more minutes.

Maybe it was initially the warmth of the sidewalk on this cool morning that enticed him from the safety of mother earth. I don't know. What I do know is that even when he was on the edge of survival, almost completely done in by his mistake—lost from that which could nurture him in a healthy way—he continued to head in the direction of death.

We love Jesus' parable of the prodigal son because in the end, the son found his way home. We love echoing the words of the father in the parable when he says, "For this son of mine was dead, but now he is alive; he was lost, but now he has been found." In the parable the son ran out of money, hit a wall of desperation, and fortunately found his way back home before meeting with any additional difficulties. What if his inheritance had been a little bigger? What if his money supply would have allowed him to remain in his life of decadence a little longer? Would he have survived to return home for a happy ending?

Unfortunately, once we've left the relative safety of healthy living and been seduced to the *dark side* we find ourselves taking all kinds of risks to get more of whatever seduced us in the first place. When we're in the middle of it we often don't realize we're headed further from health and safety and closer to heartache and destruction. The longer we stay in the dark the more risks we take, with each one potentially leading to despair and death. Even when others who love us try to intervene it may be difficult to hear their warning if we're already in the midst of sinful, unhealthy living. Like a dehydrated worm on the hot sidewalk of life, we may even know we're dying, but can't see our way back home because we're just in too far.

So here's the good news. First, we need to be careful anytime we find our self risking stepping away from what we know to be healthy into something that our radar tells us could be potentially harmful to our self or others—even if our brain is also screaming that it sounds fun and exciting. Sin can be very seductive, and quickly overcoming. (Talk to the earthworm.) Second, God is listening, even when we can't see our way back home from

"... *he was lost* ..."

where we are. God will show us the next step if we ask. Third, we are called by God to help others find their way back.

I pray that God will help me find my way and also help me assist others to find their way back home. How about you?

(PS—This morning after taking the photo I scooped up the earthworm on a seedpod and deposited him back in the grass.)

98

"... carry my body with you ..."

"Moses took the body of Joseph with him, as Joseph had made the Israelites solemnly promise to do. Joseph had said, When God rescues you, you must carry my body with you from this place." (Exodus 13:19)

"... carry my body with you..."

I LOVE THE WAY God sends me messages. I rarely go looking for a photo or thought for inspiration; instead, they come to me. Yesterday I walked out of the church office and there sitting on the window sill about twenty feet from the door was this little critter. I'm not a bird expert but I knew from the spots and the beginnings of red feathers that it was a fledgling robin not long out of the nest. We shared sort of an awkward moment, with neither of us really knowing what to do next. He decided not to fly away (as most older birds would have done) so I decided to go get my camera. He was gracious enough to wait long enough for me to return and snap a few photos before deciding we'd had our moment and flew off. It's a rather confident pose he's striking, isn't it?

This not-long-from-the nest young robin got me to thinking about all the departures that are soon to happen. Seems like it's the season for leaving—high school and college graduations, weddings, moves timed to coincide with school-year endings, etc. It occurs to me that there are good and not so good departures.

Some departures are well-planned, long-anticipated and feel like we're moving toward or through something, maybe the next chapter of our lives. Others are like flights in the night, more like acts of desperation, and may feel like we're simply running away from something. Hopefully our departures are more like the former than the latter. Hopefully our departures allow us to step forth into a new opportunity with the blessings of those who have helped to nurture us in the previous chapter of our lives. Hopefully we can leave the nest with a sense of both a blessing to experience new freedom as well as a sense of our roots and the blessings that flow from that.

I will never forget the day my father dropped me off for my first day of college. My mother had to work that day so my father and I made the trip alone. During high school Dad and I had suffered through our *moments* with some fierce arguing that upset my mother at times. I was struggling to be in the nest while I was leaving the nest, and he was struggling to help me do both. It wasn't always a pretty scene.

On this first day of college he helped me carry my things into my new dorm room, took me to lunch, and then drove me back to the dorm. We stood beside the car to say goodbye. He extended his hand and said, "Well son, your a man now and on your own." I shook his hand and we parted.

Now don't get the impression he abandoned me. Quite the contrary, from time to time he stopped on his weekly business route through the college town to take me to dinner. On weekends with a home football game he and Mom came to see me in the marching band—and bring more food. On breaks he stopped to give me a ride back home. As he said, I was on my own—I had left the nest—but I carried him with me. His love saw to that.

Things were different after that handshake. We never really argued again. Instead, on several occasions in his absence I would be in the middle of doing something like building a deck and hear his voice say over my shoulder, "Don't you think you ought to give it one more nail just to be on the safe side?" It was years later before I realized that the handshake that day was more than a goodbye—it was a blessing. I believe the best departures happen with a blessing—a goodbye that acknowledges the freedom to move on in such a way that it allows the departing one to carry the nurturing caretakers of the nest with him or her.

I believe that when Moses and the Israelites left Egypt carrying the bones of Joseph, it represented more than the fulfillment of an old man's wish to be buried in his homeland. I believe it also meant they left carrying the divine blessing of the one who had and would continue to nurture them. To leave carrying a blessing is divine, even better, the blessing of the Divine.

I pray that in all departures with others, whether I'm leaving or being left, I will offer the blessings God and others have offered me. How about you?

99

"... a place of safety ..."

"The Lord is a refuge for the oppressed, a place of safety in times of trouble." (Psalm 9:9)

SOME OF YOU ARE saying right about now, "Hey, I've seen this picture before!" That's because you're looking at a part of the harbor in Rockport,

Massachusetts with a red fishing shack in the middle known as, "Motif #1." The Rockport natives advertise it to be the most photographed and painted building in America. (This is actually a reproduction. The original was blown away by the blizzard of 1978.)

I served as the pastor of the Rockport United Methodist Church from 1984–89 while I was doing my doctoral work in pastoral counseling at Boston University. Captain Ted and his family were part of the church. Captain Ted owned a large boat that he used for tourist sightseeing trips, whale watches, and charter fishing trips. I remember him telling stories about the frustration of tourists when they would visit the dock and find the ship tied up with a sign indicating there were no trips that day. The tourists were frustrated because the water in the harbor looked perfectly calm. They'd often demand, "Why aren't you sailing?" Captain Ted would then instruct the landlubbers on how the harbor water might seem calm enough but the waves out at sea were running at three to five feet, enough to make the strongest of them run for the rails and bellow the blues of seasickness!

Safety is often one of those things like trust. We take it for granted until we lose it. Safety is one of our most important needs. If a child develops without a sense of safety she or he will most likely be charged and scarred by tremendous anxiety. Then, life can seem like a chaotic nightmare. The same can be said for adults if they lose a sense of safety—physical, emotional, and spiritual safety.

We cannot control what's outside the entrance to the harbor. We are subjected to stresses and crises that sometimes seemingly come from nowhere like rogue waves in the dark of the night. None of us is immune to the poundings we sometimes face outside the harbor. In order to withstand and endure all that we must encounter in our day-to-day journeys, we need that safe harbor as well.

The safe harbor might be the warm embrace of a trusted partner or friend. As children it's the loving, nurturing embrace of adults who love us that helps make it okay to leave the safety of that *harbor* and voyage to new destinations. It's also the knowledge that we can return to that *harbor* or take the memories of that *harbor* with us to find new *safe harbors* that also makes it possible to journey forth.

Spiritually we need to know that God provides our ultimate safety. We need to experience the presence of God's loving embrace in order to know that whatever storms may come, we can never be torn from God's loving grasp. God's gift of divine love in Christ offers us the assurance of an eternal safe harbor. The awareness of that ultimate safety, the living into that ultimate safety helps us physically, emotionally, and spiritually survive the storms of today. God's love is not just an assurance of a heavenly safe harbor. It is the experience of a present source of relief as well.

Frankly, I'm concerned that we are being lured into more troubled waters by the promises of so many, life-consuming temptations and spending far too little time in the safe harbor of spiritual replenishment. Too much time being battered about by the pounding waves of life without spending time in the safe harbor of spiritual replenishment can lead to increased anxiety, chaos, and disintegration. I pray that God will continue to lead me to into safe harbors of spiritual replenishment with worship, fellowship, study, outreach, witness, and prayer. How about you?

100

"... stretch out their hands ..."

"If any of your people Israel, out of heartfelt sorrow, stretch out their hands in prayer toward this Temple, hear their prayer. Listen to them in your home in heaven, forgive them, and help them." (I Kings 8:38–39)

"... stretch out their hands..."

PATTI CAME UPON THIS tree during a recent hike we were taking together and called me over to it. She said she thought it might make a good *Wednesday Wonderings*. I guess after awhile I've managed to get some of you *wondering* along with me. Anyway, she was right, it is ripe for a *Wonderings*.

It looks like this tree was somehow bent over several years ago. Instead of breaking, it caught on one of its branches and used it as a support against the rocks. Then, the tree did exactly what it needed to do in order to survive. It stretched its limbs toward the sky to catch the sun. It was difficult for me to find the right angle to take the photo and do the tree justice. It bends up and down horizontally along the rock for about forty feet and then dramatically turns vertical to join it's branches in the canopy with its more vertically oriented neighbors. I don't know how the tree got into such difficulty and remained bent over. I do know that had it not found a way to stretch its limbs toward the sun, it most likely would have died.

The quote from the book of I Kings in the Old Testament is part of the dedication service of the Temple Solomon built in Jerusalem. It became the residing place for God on earth. Solomon offered this prayer because he knew on that day of dedication the sun would not set before he and his people would have sinned again. For one reason or another they would hurt each other and God.

The ways they could (and we can) hurt each other were and remain endless. Sometimes we find others and our own selves so bloodied and bruised physically, emotionally, and spiritually that it's difficult to determine how it all started in the first place. Like the bent over tree, we may not know or be able to explain how it all happened, but our need is the same. We have to find a way back to the source of life-giving hope that we require for healing and hope. Renewal came for the tree when it found the sun. For us, renewal happens when we find our way back to God.

Solomon knew that God would respond to heartfelt repentance—not shallow confession, but heartfelt repentance. Jesus confirmed that with his presence and love. Sometimes we get so caught up in trying to explain how we got *bent over* by unhealthy living (sin) that we miss or put-off the opportunity for healing. At some point in our healing it's helpful to know how we got *bent over* in order to avoid making decisions that might lead to future *bending*. However, we don't have to be able to explain how we got *bent over* to reach for what we need to recover and be renewed—the forgiving grace of God.

Wednesday Wonderings

I pray that when I find myself *bent over* I will remember to stretch out my hands to God in heartfelt repentance, knowing I will be heard, forgiven, and renewed. How about you?

101

"... wander off the road ..."

"If you wander off the road to the right or the left, you will hear his voice behind you saying, 'Here is the road. Follow it.'" (Isaiah 30:21)

I GUESS THERE'S NO question why they call this Grandview National Park. We stopped at the overlook last week while we were visiting the park with some friends to see the show, *Hatfields and McCoys.* Looking at the photo you'll see the railroad track that runs by the river. I couldn't help but notice what a circuitous route the train has to follow, traveling way down the valley and around the mountain just to get back to a spot not that far as the crow flies from where it began. While we were there we watched a freight train work its way along the tracks by the river's edge.

I don't know about you, but if I were traveling through the valley I'd probably be tempted to look for the shortcut. Why wander all the way around the river path if I could just cut straight up the side of the mountain and down the other side. It's definitely the shorter route (or so it seems). Think of the time I'd save! Somehow I suspect I'd regret that choice somewhere just shy of the top of that steep, rugged, densely tree and scrub-packed mountain.

Sometimes wandering off the road is fun and even exciting. Patti and I have been doing a lot of wandering in our new location. Driving down a road we'll make a turn and say, "Let's see where this street will take us." It's been a good way to get to know our new community. However, wandering off the road is not always such a good idea. Our impatience, stubbornness, or pride can cause us to veer off the road of healthy living that God has established. We give into thoughts like, "I know myself better than anyone else. I'll do it my way." We give into those thoughts and sometimes find ourselves halfway up that mountain beginning to realize maybe we shouldn't have veered off the road.

". . . wander off the road . . ."

Maybe someone else, maybe God, really did know the better way even if the road was longer or more circuitous than we would have chosen. Faith requires that we follow sometimes even when we would rather choose our own road over the mountain. Faith requires we remember that God really does know the way, even when we are convinced we know a better road.

"If you wander off the road to the right or the left, you will hear his voice behind you saying, 'Here is the road. Follow it.'" The prophet Isaiah reminds us that God has a road for us to follow, and even if we're halfway up that mountain we insisted on climbing instead of following God's road, listen, and we can hear God's voice leading us back. I pray that God will help me resist the temptation to veer off the road and listen for the Holy Spirit to guide me back when I do. How about you?

102

"... power over the fish, the birds..."

"Then God said, 'And now we will make human beings; they will be like us and resemble us. They will have power over the fish, the birds, and all animals, domestic and wild, large and small.' So God created human beings, making them to be like himself. He created them male and female, blessed them, and said, 'Have many children, so that your descendants will live all over the earth and bring it under their control.

"*. . . power over the fish, the birds . . .*"

I am putting you in charge of the fish, the birds, and all the wild animals.'" (Genesis 1:26–28)

Last week I made a quick stop at a local pond and began to walk the perimeter. I paused on the path when I noticed that a pair of geese had occupied the same nest I had watched the previous year. I was the only hiker on the trail so the male stood patiently to the side watching me intently. After I stood quietly for a while only about twenty feet from the nest the female decided I was safe enough, so she stood up to *feather her nest* a little more. It was then I was able to see that at least one or two eggs were already incubating beneath her. I still don't know what got into me, but when she sat back on the eggs I kept my camera focused on her and began to hum a lullaby. Then it happened . . . The goose cocked her head at me, clearly interested in and responding to the song I was humming.

I'm accustomed to my dogs responding to me, but I've only seen geese as critters that run away from me. Suddenly this one was *interested*. As strange as it may sound, it was a simple gesture, but a sacred moment. Somehow that turn of her head sent a chill down my spine, reminding me that we share a sacred connection with life—not a connection we had made, but rather, a connection with which we had been endowed by our Creator and suddenly rediscovered.

Wednesday Wonderings

We are not simply created for connection or to connect—we are created in connection. Our sacred connections don't have to be made, they have to be re-discovered, celebrated, and cherished. It makes a big difference in our lives if we live basically as loners who tolerate connections when necessary versus creatures of God seeking to discover and cherish our connectedness. We'll never succeed at getting connection-tolerating folks to care for one another and our environment if we simply sell it as something we're supposed to do, better do, or have to do. We first have to help folks discover their basic sacred connectedness.

I care because I feel the loving connection with my God who created me in connection and has sustained me in those connections with comfort, forgiveness, and hope. Sacred connection comes first—then caring that reaches forth from connection. Look for the connections and listen for the Spirit of God to speak to you of sacred connectedness—even if it comes from an inquisitive goose! I pray that God will continue to speak to me of sacred connections. I need the chills . . . How about you?

103

"... changes rocks into pools of water ..."

"Tremble, earth, at the Lord's coming, at the presence of the God of Jacob, who changes rocks into pools of water and solid cliffs into flowing springs." (Psalm 114:7–8)

WHEN WE THINK OF rocks we think of strength, something so strong that we can use them for foundations of homes and skyscrapers. As I watched the waves pound these rocks on the coast of Maine I was reminded that the rocks were once part of the cliff where I was standing. With time and great power the waves and wind had whittled away at the cliff leaving rocks scattered along the way. With more time the rocks will be reduced to the sand at the base of the cliff, and with more time . . .

I am always in awe of the power of the wind and waves. I am also in awe of the power of God to create and renew. Imagine, power such that the Psalmist cries, "Tremble, earth, at the Lord's coming, at the presence of the God of Jacob, who changes rocks into pools of water and solid cliffs into flowing springs."

Sometimes it's hard to see the hand of God at work. When we're in the midst of heartache and crisis it can be especially difficult to see God using the power of divine love to mold and make each day and moment for our good. Yet other times, when life actually is going pretty well, can also be difficult occasions to see the hand of God at work because we get comfortable and forget to look. Once we forget to look its easy for us to forget to believe—that the power of God is behind every part of our lives.

When I'm counseling with folks in the initial stages of recovery from an addiction I always warn them that one of their most vulnerable times for relapse is when everything is going well. That's because they quit doing the things that were helping them stay on the road to recovery. They quit focusing on the disciplines they were taught that help keep them safe and healthy. They quit *looking*, if you will—and then comes the fall.

The power of God is real and available for our healing and transformation, and for the transformation of the world. God has never stopped offering this power—we've only quit looking. If rocks can be transformed so can we. God's love in Christ is real and available. I pray that God will keep me looking. How about you?

104

"... mere mortals..."

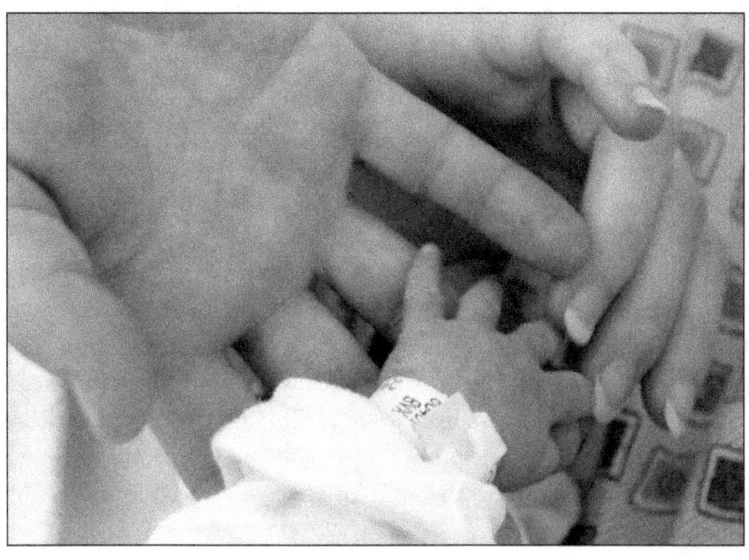

"When I look at the sky, which you have made, at the moon and the stars, which you set in their places—what are human beings, that you think of them; mere mortals, that you care for them? Yet you made them inferior only to yourself; you crowned them with glory and honor." (Psalm 8:3–5)

Wednesday Wonderings

It's almost midnight but I found that I could not finish this day without *wondering*. I could not conclude one of the most important days of my life without reflecting upon its impact on my spiritual journey. I could not end this day without saying, "Thank you, God!" At 3:30 this morning Patti and I received the telephone call from our daughter-in-law letting us know that her and our son's first child (and our first grandchild) was about to be born. We jumped in our car and drove the six hours to the hospital, missing the birth of our granddaughter, but arriving in time for many other *firsts*. Needless to say, it has been an exhilarating day!

I couldn't help but think about the Psalm as I watched our granddaughter with her parents. There was nothing "mere" about this child or moment! I believe that's exactly what the Psalmist was trying to remind us. How can anyone be part of such an event and not be swept up in the grandeur and glory of God that we are privileged to glimpse from time to time? Today, once more, I stared into the face of a newborn and saw reflected back the majesty and wonder of the Divine. This time instead of one of my own newborn children, it was my grandchild. It feels really good to write that so allow me to indulge myself by writing it one more time—*my grandchild!*

It is also a privilege to see my granddaughter bathed and held in the same love by her parents that we have given her parents. We live in a world where we're keenly aware of the mistakes we make. I know Patti and I have made our share as parents. However, as I watched our son and daughter-in-law today, I was blessed to see some of what we apparently got right. It made me smile, laugh, and cry for joy. I know as Christians we spend a lot of time reflecting on our failures and need for forgiveness—as we should. However, I believe there are a lot of times when God is smiling because God sees us loving like we've been loved in Christ! That's a lot to celebrate!

I pray that God will help me continue to appreciate and celebrate all the times we get it right together and love like we've been loved in Christ! How about you?

www.ingramcontent.com/pod-product-compliance
Lightning Source LLC
Chambersburg PA
CBHW050349230426
43663CB00010B/2052